STONE CIRCLES
IN BRITAIN

DAVID J. EVANS

AMBERLEY

First published 2024

Amberley Publishing, The Hill, Stroud
Gloucestershire GL5 4EP

www.amberley-books.com

British Library Cataloguing in Publication Data.
A catalogue record for this book is available from the British Library.

ISBN 978 1 3981 0592 8 (print)
ISBN 978 1 3981 0593 5 (ebook)

Typesetting by SJmagic DESIGN SERVICES, India.
Printed in Great Britain.

CONTENTS

ACKNOWLEDGEMENTS

The author and publisher would like to thank the following people/organisations for permission to use copyright material in this book: Cambridge University Press, Canmore (Historic Environment Scotland), Cornwall Council, English Heritage (Historic England Executive Non-Departmental Public Body) and Coflein (online database for the National Monuments Record of Wales) for archaeology reports and historic information. The author and publisher would also like to thank Andy Burnham and contributors of The Megalithic Portal, Julian Cope and contributors to The Modern Antiquarian, contributors to Wikipedia Stone Circle web pages, www.gridreferencefinder.com and www.openstreetmap.org for various pointers to the sites. I would also like to express my gratitude to all of the friendly farmers/land owners and 'fellow Stone Botherers' for sharing valued information along my journey. A special thank you also to Nick Grant from Amberley Publishing for guidance and commissioning this book. Every attempt has been made to seek permission for copyright material used. However, if we have inadvertently used copyright material without permission/acknowledgement we apologise and we will make the necessary correction at the first opportunity. Notes: this book includes analysis, grid references and photography for my visits to the stone circles. Any photographs not included in this book along with maps, coordinates and directions for your explorations can be found on my website www.cozmicdave.com. I sincerely hope the information I have provided gives you, the reader, an insight and provides curiosity, enjoyment and pleasure while reading it. May it encourage one to continue researching and exploring the magic and mystery of stone circles and many other historic sites that await you. With best wishes, David J. Evans BA (Hons).

Callanish I.

INTRODUCTION

What Are Stone Circles?

Stone circles are prehistoric monuments built during the Middle Neolithic and Early Bronze Ages, more commonly known as the Megalithic Period. The oldest sites originate from Turkey, dating back to more than 1000 BC, Israel 7000 BC, and Portugal 5000 BC. Other sites, especially in north-western France, date back to 4500 BC. In 4000 BC agriculture was introduced to Great Britain from Europe. However, it was not until 2500–3700 BC that stone circles appeared in the United Kingdom. Recent carbon dating tells us that the first sites were Callanish I (2900 BC) in the Outer Hebrides, the Stones of Stennes (3400 BC) and the Ring of Brodgar (2500 BC) in the Orkney Islands. The oldest stone circle in England is Castlerigg (3000 BC). A stone circle called Waun Maun (3600 BC) did exist in the Preseli Hills, West Wales. It was thought to be the original Bluestonehenge Stone Circle which now stands inside Stonehenge, however, recent investigations since 2021 have concluded there was no definite connection. Yet there is no doubt that the Bluestones did actually come from nearby quarries.

Stone Circles and Their Purposes

We will never know the truth of why or even how stone circles were built, or for what purpose they served. All the evidence we have is from the words of historians and the findings from archaeologists. Historians state that the principal reason for building these monuments was mainly for tribal gatherings, where they performed rituals and worshipping of the heavens above. There is possibly some truth in what they say because each stone belonging to the circles are precisely aligned to mark solar and lunar events, as well as pivotal points in the seasons such as the spring equinox, summer solstice and winter solstice. Archaeologists provide us with evidence of burials and cremations within these sites, which suggests that stone circles were also an early form of churches and cemeteries. However, through research and personal visits to the stone circles documented here in this book, my assumption is that stone circles were probably calendars used for agricultural purposes. Farmers would have needed some indication of date and time as to when to begin planting seeds to grow food. It was indeed they, the farmers, who introduced stone circles to Great Britain. These sites were then later adapted for other purposes.

Design

In the beginning, some of these circles (such as Woodhenge and Stonehenge) were made of tall wooden posts, which stood perfectly upright and were set deep into the ground. Stone circles were introduced soon after and either replaced the wooden circles or combined them. This was not the case at Woodhenge, however, as no evidence of any stones exists. There are various designs of stone circles, some of which are almost perfectly round or oval (elliptical). Some have one or more rings of standing or laid-down stones (in most cases having fallen) inside or outside of the circle, occasionally surrounded by earthwork features such as enclosing banks and ditches. Sometimes avenues of standing stones (stone rows) are attached to the circle, such as Avebury Henge, Callanish I, Hingston Hill, Ringmoor and Sourton Tor. As the megaliths progressed through the years to 3500 BCE, these designs became more elaborate, not only with the construction of stone circles but also the dolmens, burial chambers (cairns) and long barrows. These monuments were usually built close to the stone circles and aligned with precision to the sunrise, sunsets and other planetary events. At some sites, especially in north-western Great Britain, they were even placed within the circle.

Another type of stone circle is the 'recumbent' design. There are over 200 recumbent stone circles that only exist in north-east Scotland and the counties of Cork and Kerry, south-west Ireland. Ninety-nine of them are located in Aberdeenshire alone. This type of design incorporates a large stone block laid on its side between the two tallest standing stones (flankers) positioned on the south-west side of the circle. Because of their alignments with the arc of the southern moon, it suggests these recumbent stone circles were built for rituals and moon ceremonies.

Inner section of Kirkton of Bourtie Recumbent Stone Circle.

LIST OF STONE CIRCLES INCLUDING ALTERNATIVE NAMES

STONE CIRCLES IN ENGLAND

East Midlands: Derbyshire

Arbor Low (alternative names: Arbelow, Arbor Low 1, Eordburg Hlaw)

Barbrook Stone Circles (alternative names: Barbrook 1, Barbrook 2, Barbrook 3. Barbrook 3 is also known as Owler Bar)

Doll Tor Stone Circle (alternative names: The Six Stones)

Froggatt Edge Stone Circle (alternative names: Stoke Flat)

Hordron Edge Stone Circle (alternative names: Hordron Circle, Seven Stones of Hordron Edge)

Nine Ladies Stone Circle (alternative names: Nine Ladies of Stanton Moor, Stanton Moor II)

Nine Stones Close Stone Circle (alternative name: The Grey Ladies)

West Midlands: Shropshire

Mitchell's Fold Stone Circle (alternative names: Medgel's Fold, Mitchells Fold)

Pen Y Wern Hill Stone Circle (alternative name: Pen Y Wern)

North-west England: Cumbria

Burnmoor Stone Circles (alternative names for each circle: Brat's Hill also known as Burn Moor, Eskdale; Low Longrigg NE, Low Longrigg SW, White Moss NE also known as Burn Moor; White Moss SW)

Castlerigg Stone Circle (alternative names: The Carles, Druid's Circle, Keswick)

The Cockpit Stone Circle (alternative names: One of Moor Divock Group)

Long Meg & Her Daughters Stone Circle (alternative names: Long Meg, Maughanby Circle)

Swinside Stone Circle (alternative names: Sunkenkirk, Sunken Kirk)

South-east England: Oxfordshire

The King's Men (alternative names: Rollendrith, Rollright Stones, Rowldrich, The Rollrights)

South-west England: Avon & Somerset

Porlock Stone Circle (alternative names: Porlock Allotment, Porlock Common, Monument No. 36228)

Stanton Drew Stone Circles I, II, & III (alternative names: Stanton Drew NE Circle, Stanton Drew SSW, The Great Circle, The Weddings at Stanton)

Withypool Stone Circle (alternative names: Withypool Hill Circle)

Cornwall

Altarnun Stone Circle (alternative names: Nine Stones, Nine Stones of Altarnun)

Boscawen-Un Stone Circle (alternative names: Boscawen Un, Boscawen ûn, Boskawen-Un, Nine Maidens, Naw-Whoors)

Boskednan Stone Circle (alternative names: Ding Dong, Nine Maidens, Nine Maidens of Boskednan, Nine Stones of Boskednan)

Craddock Moor Stone Circle (alternative name: Craddock Circle)

Duloe Stone Circle

Emblance Downs Stone Circles (alternative names for each circle: Emblance Down NW, Emblance Down SE, King Arthur's Down SE, King Arthur's Down NW, Leaze NW)

Fernacre Stone Circle

Goodaver Stone Circle

The Hurlers Stone Circles (alternative name: Hurlers)

Leaze Stone Circle

Louden Stone Circle (alternative names: Louden Hill Stone Circle, Candra Hill)

Merry Maidens Stone Circle (alternative names: Boleigh Circle, Boleit Circle, Dans Maen, Dans Mean, Dawn's Men, Dawns-mên, Dons Meyn, Rosmodreuy Circle, Rosmoddress, Rosemodress Stone Circle)

Stannon Stone Circle

Stripple Stones Stone Circle (alternative name: SX14357521)

Tregeseal Stone Circle (alternative names: Carn Kenidzhek, Dancing Stones, Merry Maidens, Nine Maidens, Tregeseal East)

Trippet Stones Stone Circle

Devon

Brisworthy Stone Circle (alternative name: Monument No. 438683)

Fernworthy Stone Circle (alternative name: Froggymead, Monument No. 443854)

Grey Wethers Stone Circles I & II (alternative names: Gray Wethers, The Greywethers, Monument No. 443916, Turner G2)

Hingston Hill Stone Circle (alternative names: Down Tor, Hingston Stone Row)

Hexworthy Stone Circle (alternative names: Down Ridge, Monument No. 443043)

Little Hound Tor Stone Circle (alternative names: Monument No. 443694, Turner G11, White Moor Stone Circle, Whitemoorstone Down Stone Circle)

Merrivale Stone Circle (alternative names: Monument No. 440044, Turner G14)

Nine Maidens Stone Circle (alternative names: Belstone Stone Circle, Grinsell Belstone 1, Nine Stones, Seventeen Brothers, Turner Stone Circle G23)

Ringmoor Down Stone Circle (alternative name: Ringmoor Down).

Scorhill Stone Circle (alternative names: Gidleigh Stone Circle, Monument No. 443556, Turner G6 Butler map 38.8)

Sherberton Stone Circle (alternative names: Turner G5, Monument No. 443298)

Shovel Down Stone Circle (alternative names: Fourfold Circle, Monument No. 443527, Shovel Down NW)

Sourton Tors Stone Circle (alternative names: Corn Ridge Stone Circle, Sowton Tors, Turner G3)

Soussons Common Cairn Circle (alternative names: Butler Soussons Plantation V2 24.2.6, Ephraim's Pinch, Grinsell Manaton 9, Turner D2, Dixon D16, Runnage Circle)

Sittaford Stone Circle

Yellowmead Stone Circle (alternative names: G30 Turner, Piskie House, Sheepstor 4 (Grinsell), Sheeps Tor, Sheep's Tor, Yellowmead Down, Yellowmead Multiple Stone Circle)

Dorset

Hampton Down Stone Circle (alternative names: Hampton Stone Circle, Monument No. 450399)

Kingston Russell Stone Circle (alternative names: The Gorwell Circle)

Nine Stones (alternative names: Nine Ladies, The Devil's Nine Stones, The Nine Stones of Winterbourne Abbas)

Rempstone Stone Circle (alternative name: Monument No. 456759)

Gloucestershire

East Wood Henge (alternative names: Embanked Stone Circle near Madgett's Farm, Forest of Dean Stone Circle, Monument No. 43410)

Wiltshire

Avebury Down Stone Circle (alternative names: Avebury 64a, Monument No. 221596, Pennings Bell Barrow, Penning Stone Circle)

Avebury Henge (alternative names: Waledich)

Bluestonchenge (alternative names: Bluehenge, Riverhenge, West Amesbury Henge)

Coate Stone Circle (alternative name: Day House Lane)

Falkner's Stone Circle

Langdean Stone Circle (alternative names: Cow Down, Langdean Bottom, Little Avebury)

Stonehenge (alternative names: Chorea Gigantum, Cor y Cewri Stan-heng, The Giant's Dance)

Winterbourne Bassett Stone Circle

STONE CIRCLES IN SCOTLAND

North-east Scotland: Aberdeenshire

Aikey Brae Stone Circle (alternative names: Parkhouse Hill, Aiky Brae)

Berrybrae Recumbent Stone Circle

Cullerie Stone Circle (alternative names: Cullerlie, Cullerlie of Echt, Standing Stones of Cullerlie, Standing Stones of Echt, Standing Stones Farm, Leuchar Moss)

Easter Aquhorthies Recumbent Stone Circle (alternative names: East Aquhorties, Easter Aquhorthies)

Dunnideer Recumbent Stone Circle (alternative name: Dunnydeer Farm)

Eslie the Greater Recumbent Stone Circle (alternative names: Esslie Major, Eslie South, West Mullo)

Eslie the Lesser Stone Circle (alternative names: Esslie Minor, Eslie North, West Mullo, Esslie the Less)

Image Wood Stone Circle (alternative name: Aboyne Stone Circle)

Kirkton of Bourtie Recumbent Stone Circle (alternative name: Kirktown of Bourtie)

Loanhead of Daviot Recumbent Stone Circle (alternative names: Loanhead, Stone Circle and Enclosed Cremation Cemetery)

Loudon Wood Recumbent Stone Circle (alternative name: Pitfour Circle)

Midmar Kirk Recumbent Stone Circle (alternative names: Midmar Church, Midmar Graveyard, Christchurch)

The Nine Stanes Stone Circle (alternative names: Garrol Wood, Garrol Hill, Mulloch Wood)

Stonehead Recumbent Stone Circle (alternative names: Whitebrow, Stonehouse)

Sunhoney Stone Circle (alternative names: Seanhinny, Dunecht Estate)

Tomnagorn Stone Circle (alternative name: Tamnagorn)

Tomnaverie Recumbent Stone Circle (alternative names: Mill of Wester Coull, The Tomnaverie, Tarland Burn)

Yonder Bognie (alternative name: Yonder Bognie Warden)

Angus

Balgarthno Stone Circle (alternative names: The Devil's Stones, Farm of Corn, Gourdie Stone Circle, 850m South of Myrekirk, Liff Railway Station, Myrekirk, The Nine Stanes of Invergowrie)

Colmeallie Stone Circle

Templelands Stone Circle (alternative name: Auchterhouse)

The Orkney Isles

Ring of Brodgar (alternative names: Ring of Brogar, Ness of Brodgar, Circle at Stennis)

Stones of Stennes (alternative names: Temple of the Moon, Temple of the Sun, Ring of Stenness, Stan Stanes, Old Charlies, Howerstadgarth)

Perthshire

Croft Moraig Stone Circle (alternative name: Croftmoraig)

North-west Scotland: Argyle and Bute

Temple Wood Stone Circles I and II

Dumfries and Galloway

Torhouse Stone Circle (alternative names: Torhouse Stones, Torhousekie, King Gauldus's Tomb)

Isle of Arran

Auchagallon Stone Circle
Machrie Moor 1 Stone Circle
Machrie Moor 2 Stone Circle
Machrie Moor 3 Stone Circle
Machrie Moor 4 Stone Circle
Machrie Moor 5 Stone Circle
Machrie Moor 11 Stone Circle
Moss Farm Road Stone Circle & Cairn

The Outer Hebrides: Isle of Lewis

Achmore Stone Circle (alternative name: Acha Mor)

Bernera Bridge Stone Circle (alternative names: Callanish VIII, Cleitir, Great Berneray, 'Tursachan' Barraglom)

Callanish Stone Circle 1 (alternative names: Calanais, Callanish I, Tursachan Callanish, Classiness)

Callanish Stone Circle 2 (alternative names: Cnoc Ceann a' Gharraidh, Knock Ceann a Gharries, Loch Roag)

Callanish Stone Circle 3 (alternative names: Cnoc Fillibhir Bheag, Cnoc Fillibhir Bheag, Knock Heliair)

Sron a' Chail Stone Circle (alternative names: Ceann Hulavig, Callanish IV, Ceann Thulabhaig, Ceann Thulabig Tursachan, Loch Roag)

Steinacleit Stone Circle (alternative names: Stein-a-cleat, Lower Shader, Siadar, Lewis Shader Steinacleit)

North Uist

Pobull Fhinn Stone Circle (alternative names: Pobuill Fhinn, Sornach Coir' Fhinn)

STONE CIRCLES IN WALES

Mid Wales

Ysbyty Cynfyn Stone Circle (alternative name: Ysptty Cynyn)

North Wales

Bryn Cader Faner Cairn Circle

Druid's Circle (alternative names: Druids Circle, Y Meini Hirion)

Eglwys Gwyddelod Stone Circle (alternative name: Irishman's Church)

Llyn Eiddew Bach III Stone Circle (alternative name: Llyn Eiddew-Bach)

Moel Ty Uchaf Stone Circle (alternative names: Moel Ty-Uchaf)

Penbedw Stone Circle (alternative names: Penbedw Park)

Tyfos Stone Circle

Powys

Cerrig Duon & The Maen Mawr Stone Circle (alternative names: Cerrig Duon)

Four Stones Circle (alternative name: The Four Kings)

Pen Y Beacon Stone Circle (alternative names: Blaenau, Pen Y Beacon)

Trecastle Mountain Stone Circles (alternative names: Mynydd Bach, Pigwn, Cerrig Y Pigwyn, Y Pigwyn)

South Wales

Gray Hill Stone Circle (alternative names: Grey Hill, Mynydd Llwyd)

West Wales

Dyffryn Syfynwy Stone Circle (alternative names: Henry's Moat, Garn Ochr, Dyffryn Circle, St Brynach's Well, St Bernac's Well, Bernard's Well)

Gors Fawr Stone Circle (alternative names: Cylch y Trallwyn)

STONE CIRCLES IN THE EAST MIDLANDS

DERBYSHIRE

Arbor Low

Arbor Low is a Neolithic site consisting of a stone circle surrounded by massive earthworks and a ditch. The stone circle is ovular in shape that has fifty large limestone blocks. There may have been forty-three stones originally, but some are now fragmented. The stones vary in size from about 5.3 feet to 7 feet (1.6 to 2.1 metres), with other monoliths between 8.6 feet 6 and 9.6 feet (2.6–2.9 metres). One of the stones stands almost upright, and the rest are all lying flat. Six smaller stones lie in the centre of the circle (known as 'the cove') and may have once been arranged in a rectangle. Surrounding the stones is an earth bank measuring approximately 295 by 279 feet (90 by 85 metres). It has a height of 6.7 feet (2 metres) with an inner ditch about 6.7 feet (2 metres) deep and 23 to 33 feet (7–10 metres) wide. There are two entries into the circle. One is at the north-west measuring 30 feet (9 metres) wide. The other entrance is at the south-east measuring 20 feet (6 metres) wide.

Arbor Low Stone Circle.

The inner bank enclosure has an area of 171 feet by 131 feet (52 by 40 metres). During the years 1901 and 1902, the site was excavated. Archaeologists found arrowheads, bone, antler tools, flint scrapers, and near the cove was human skeletal remains. There is also Gib Hill Barrow in the next field approximately 100 feet (300 metres) south-west of Arbor Low. Arbor Low Stone Circle and Gib Hill Barrow are open to the public and signposted on the Long Rake Road directly opposite Upper Oldhams Farm. The farmer charges an entrance fee of £1 per adult, but free for children. Grid reference: SK 16040 63561.

Barbrook Stone Circles

There are three Bronze Age stone circles at Barbrook situated in a field of eighty cairns on Big Moor and Ramsley Moor in the Peak District. The area is a designated Scheduled Ancient Monument. Barbrook I Stone Circle measures 42.6 feet (13 metres) in diameter and contains twelve stones surrounded by an embankment 9.85 feet (3 metres) wide. Eleven of them measure between approximately 1.9 inches and 10 inches (5 to 25 centimetres) high. The other stone is about 39.4 inches (1 metre) tall. Barbrook Stone Circles I and II are situated along the public footpath. There is a lay-by next to it on the A361 near Holmsfield. Grid reference: SK 27850 75580. Barbrook II Stone Circle is situated approximately 656 feet (200 metres) north-west from Barbrook I. The inside of the circle measures approximately 44 feet (13.4 metres) in diameter. It contains a cairn and has nine stones. One of them is possibly missing since first built. The outer rocky bank is about 11 feet (3.4 metres) wide. Grid reference: SK 27750 75820. Barbrook III is a ruined circle situated about (2 kilometres) further north from the other two stone circles. Many stones are either leaning or have fallen and hidden by the moorland. An embankment measures about 28.4 yards by 25.6 yards (26 metres by 23.5 metres) in diameter surrounds the circle. Access to Barbrook Stone Circle III is via the public footpath from the lay-by opposite a small building with green gates on the B6054 road. Grid reference: SK 28330 77280.

Barbrook I Stone Circle.

Above: Barbrook II Stone Circle.

Below: Barbrook III Stone Circle.

Doll Tor Stone Circle.

Doll Tor Stone Circle

Doll Tor is a small Bronze Age stone circle measuring approximately 19.7 feet by 14.8 feet (6 metres by 4.5 metres) in diameter. It consists of six stones about 3 feet tall. Four of them are still standing, but two larger stones have fallen. Several large boulders are standing about 33 feet (10 metres) away from the circle and are likely they are connected. Although Doll Tor has an information board at the site, it stands on private land and not open to the public, therefore asking permission to visit is strongly advised. Grid reference: SK 23830 62873.

Froggatt Edge Stone Circle

Froggatt Edge is an embanked stone circle constructed during the early Bronze Age. It stands on public land close to the Froggatt Edge footpath. The circle measures approximately 50 feet (15.3 metres) in diameter, and the bank is 6.5 feet (2 metres) wide, 37.7 feet (11.5 metres) internally. It has two entrances, one north-north-east and the other, south-south-west. Most of the stones are less than a foot in height, except for a standing stone approximately 31.2 feet (9.5 metres) tall, at the southern edge of the circle. Grid reference: SK 24960 76790.

Hordron Edge Stone Circle

Hordron Edge is a ruined Bronze Age stone circle situated 1,770 feet (540 metres) south-east of Cutthroat Bridge. It stands close to the edge of Moscar Moor overlooking the Derwent Valley. The circle measures approximately 50 feet (16 metres) in diameter and may have contained twenty-six stones originally, but today most of them are missing. All that

Hordron Edge Stone Circle.

remains are eleven stones measuring between 1.45 feet and 4 feet (45–95 centimetres) long and another three stones buried underground. Grid reference: SK 21524 86851.

Nine Ladies Stone Circle

Nine Ladies is a Bronze Age stone circle consisting of ten 'millstone grit' stones. Nine of them are still standing upright, and one stone is recumbent. Each of the standing stones measures up to 3.3 feet (1 metre) in height and the other is the same in length. The circle has a large gap at the south side. No archaeological evidence of a stone hole exists to

Nine Ladies Stone Circle.

suggest the recumbent stone once stood upright. There is also a small stone nearby called the 'King Stone' situated approximately 43.8 yards (40 metres) west-south-west of the circle. However, there is no evidence to confirm whether or not it is part of the stone circle. Nine Ladies Stone Circle is surrounded by woodland at the top of Stanton Moor. It belongs to the Stanton Estate with many public footpaths leading to the site. Permission to access is not required. Grid Reference: SK 24900 63500.

Nine Stones Close Stone Circle

Nine Stones Close is a Bronze Age stone circle situated at the edge of Harthill Moor belonging to the Stanton Estate. It measures almost 98.5 feet (30 metres) in diameter and contains only four standing stones about 5 feet (1.5 metres) tall. Five stones are missing from the circle. However, one of them is a gate post for the nearby field. Access is across the farmer's field, which has a public footpath directly opposite the entrance to Moor Farm. There is room for parking a little further along the lane. Grid Reference: SK 22500 62600.

Nine Stones Close Stone Circle.

STONE CIRCLES IN THE WEST MIDLANDS

SHROPSHIRE

Mitchell's Fold Stone Circle

Mitchell's Fold Stone Circle is a Bronze Age Scheduled Ancient Monument, owned and cared for by English Heritage. It stands at a height of 1,083 feet (330 metres) upon the south-west end of Stapeley Hill, near the small village of White Grit, south-west Shropshire. The circle may have once contained thirty stones, but today only fifteen of them remain. These stones vary in height from 10 inches to 6 feet 3 in (1.91 metres) and stand in an ellipse of 89 feet (27 metres) north-west to south-east by 82 feet (25 metres). Mitchell's Fold is signposted on the lane and has a car park at the end of the track. The stone circle is a short walk of approximately 984 feet (300 metres), heading north-east over the brow of the hill. Grid Reference: SO 30424 98375.

Pen Y Wern Hill Stone Circle

A well and truly ruined and neglected site with cairns that appears to have been a very important stone circle. Unfortunately, it has been heavily robbed over the centuries and has similarities to some of the recumbent stone circles in Scotland. Pen Y Wern Stone Circle is situated on farmland with a public footpath. At the second gate there is a standing stone and to the right is the site at the hill with four trees. Access to the site is unavailable if crops are growing. Grid Reference: SO 31300 7800.

Mitchell's Fold Stone Circle.

STONE CIRCLES IN NORTH-WEST ENGLAND

CUMBRIA

Burnmoor Stone Circles

The Burnmoor Stone Circles (Brat's Hill, White Moss (north-east and south-west) and Low Longrigg north-east and south-west) are a group of five Bronze Age stone circles situated 1 mile north of the village of Boot. Each circle is different in design and is cared for by the National Trust. There are also about a hundred and thirty-five cairns in the vicinity.

Brat's Hill Stone Circle is larger than the other four circles and measures 98.4 feet (30 metres) in diameter. It consists of approximately forty-two stones set in an irregular ring. There are five funerary cairns within it, together with two other stones. There is also a stone approximately 32.8 feet (10 metres) north-west of the circle. Grid Reference: NY 17370 02340.

White Moss Stone Circles (north-east and south-west) are situated approximately 328 feet (100 metres) to the north-west of Brat's Hill Stone Circle. The north-east stone circle contains eleven stones and measures (16 metres) in diameter. Grid Reference: NY 17300 02410. The south-west circle contains fourteen stones and measures (16.5 metres) in diameter. Each of the stone circles have cairns in the centre. Grid Reference: NY 17250 02390.

Low Longrigg Stone Circles (north-east and south-west) are situated approximately 547 yards (500 metres) to the north-west of Brat's Hill Stone Circle. The north-east stone circle is an irregular ring containing fifteen stones and measures 68.9 feet (21 metres) in diameter. It has two cairns in the centre. Grid Reference: NY 17200 02800. The south-west stone circle measures (15 metres) in diameter and contains a cairn in the centre with nine stones surrounding it. Grid Reference: NY 17200 02700.

Castlerigg Stone Circle

Castlerigg Stone Circle is one of the earliest and largest stone circles in Great Britain and Europe. It is said to have been built during the Neolithic period about 4,500 years ago, by the prehistoric farming community. In 1913 Castlerigg was given to the National Trust for protection. A single stone, approximately 3 feet (0.9 metres) high, stands at the edge of the field by a stile to the south-west of the circle. There is no evidence available to determine if the stone is a part of the Castlerigg circle. The only information known is that in the early twentieth century a farmer found it just below the surface. He then dug up the stone and erected it. Grid Reference: NY 29143 23630.

Above: Castlerigg Stone Circle.

Below: Possible outlaying stone belonging to Castlerigg Stone Circle.

The altar inside Castlerigg Stone Circle.

The Cockpit

The Cockpit is a Bronze Age stone circle built on the north-west side of Moor Divock overlooking the Ullswater Valley, near Pooley Bridge in the Lake District, Cumbria. It measures approximately 88.6 feet (27 metres) in diameter, consisting of seventy-five stones which are less than a metre in height. Some remain standing and some fallen. A small area within the circle provides evidence of the possibility it contained an inner ring of stones. Grid Reference: NY 48300 22300.

The Cockpit Stone Circle.

Long Meg and Her Daughters Stone Circle.

Long Meg and Her Daughters Stone Circle

Long Meg and Her Daughters is a Neolithic stone circle. It is the third largest site in England containing fifty-nine stones and measures approximately 300 by 360 feet (91.5 metres by 110 metres) in diameter. The mother stone (Long Meg) is the tallest at 12 feet (3.6 metres) high. It is a red-sandstone monolith and stands 80 feet (25 metres) to the south-west of the circle. The rest of the smaller ones are known as the daughter stones. The stone circle is divided by a trackway leading to the farmer's house. There is a parking area and free entry. Anyone visiting this site please be aware that cows live in the open field, and sometimes they gather amongst the stones. Grid Reference: NY 57100 37200.

Swinside Stone Circle

Swinside is an impressive stone circle built during the Neolithic and Bronze Ages. It measures approximately 93.8 feet (26.8 metres) in diameter. There are fifty-five stones which have various heights up to 10 feet (3 metres) tall. It may have contained sixty stones when first built. At the south-eastern side of the circle, two portal stones are marking

Swinside Stone Circle.

the entrance. The space between them measures 7 feet (2.1 metres) wide. Swinside Stone Circle is accessible via a long walk along a trackway leading to a farm. Public cars are not allowed on the trackway, therefore parking next to the bridge on the lane is advisable. Grid Reference: SD 17200 88200.

STONE CIRCLES IN SOUTH-EAST ENGLAND

OXFORDSHIRE

The King's Men Stone Circle

The King's Men Stone Circle is a part of the Rollright complex situated next to the road between the border counties of Oxfordshire and Warwickshire. It is a Late Neolithic/Early Bronze Age monument, as construction of the site began sometime in 2,500 BC. The monument consists of seventy-seven limestones in a ring approximately 108 feet (33 metres) in diameter. Stones are missing at the entrance to the south-east, which suggests the circle may have originally contained more than a hundred stones and were probably stolen over the ages to build bridges and walls. The stones are badly weathered and vary in size. The tallest is almost 10 feet (3 metres) high. The Rollrights complex stands between the borders of Oxfordshire and Warwickshire at 'Cross Hands Lane'. It can be accessed from the lay-by. Grid Reference: SP 29579 30868.

The King's Men Stone Circle.

STONE CIRCLES IN SOUTH-WEST ENGLAND

AVON & SOMERSET

Porlock Stone Circle

Porlock is a ruined stone circle built during the Late Neolithic and Early Bronze Ages. It is one of only two stone circles still surviving in this area (the other is the Withypool Stone Circle). The circle measures 79 feet (24 metres) in diameter and contains thirteen 'green micaceous' sandstones. The number of stones that stood when first built is unknown. Porlock Stone Circle is situated in a corner of farmland next to the hedgerow along Mill Lane. Most of the stones are hidden by the overgrowth but part of the circle can be seen from the gate entrance. Grid Reference: SS 84510 44670.

Stanton Drew Stone Circles

Stanton Drew is a Late Neolithic to Early Bronze Age monument constructed between 3000 and 2000 BCE. It is the second-largest stone circle site in Britain, measuring 371 feet (113 metres) in diameter. The site consists of three stone circles: a large one (known as the Great Circle) and two smaller ones next to it. The Great Stone Circle once contained thirty

Stanton Drew Stone Circle I.

Above: Stanton Drew Stone Circle II.

Below: Stanton Drew Stone Circle III.

stones, but today only twenty-six of them remain standing. The two smaller stone circles are in the same field. One of them is called the North East Stone Circle and is situated next to the Great Circle. The other is approximately 450 feet away and called the South West Stone Circle. There are also more stones in the village called the 'Cove', next to The Druids Arms Inn car park. It is uncertain whether or not the Cove monument is part of the Stanton Drew Stone Circles. However, a standing stone named 'Hautville's Quoit' can be found just off the B3130 and is aligned to the Great Stone Circle. Stanton Drew has a small parking area directly opposite the main entrance. There is also a collection box for donations towards upkeep of the site. Grid Reference: ST 59990 63280.

Withypool Stone Circle

This stone circle stands on the south-western Exmoor slope of Withypool Hill, 733 yards (670 metres) to the east-south-east of Portford Bridge, near the village of Withypool, Somerset. It was built during the Late Neolithic and Early Bronze Ages and measures approximately 119.6 feet 6 (36.4 metres) in diameter. It may have contained around a hundred gritstones, all of them spaced about 3.3 feet (1 metre) apart when first constructed. All of the stones are roughly the same size, measuring approximately 4 inches (10 cm) in height, 1 foot (30 centimetres) in width and 4 inches (10 centimetres) in depth. The tallest is about 1.8 feet (0.5 metres). Today only thirty stones remain. Sadly, many of them are broken and incomplete or buried under the overgrowth. Grid Reference: SS 83827 34313.

Withypool Stone Circle.

CORNWALL

Altarnun Stone Circle

Altarnun is a Bronze Age stone circle owned and managed by English Heritage. It is the smallest stone circle on Bodmin Moor, measuring 49 feet (15 metres) in diameter. In 1889, the circle was restored when only two of the stones were found standing. Today, the circle has eight granite stones, which are now upright surrounding a standing stone in the centre. The stones are placed irregularly with a gap where another stone may have once stood. The tallest stone is 4.2 feet (1.3 metres). There is also a flat triangular-shaped stone that lies at the base of the outer ring of stones. Altarnun Stone Circle involves a long trek along the public pathway from Clitters Plantation to East Moor. There is no other easy route to reach it. Grid Reference: SX 23610 78140.

Boscawen-Un Stone Circle

Boscawen-Un is an elliptical stone circle with an axis measuring 81.7 feet by 71.8 feet (24.9 metres and 21.9 metres). It was constructed in the Late Neolithic to Early Bronze Ages and consists of twenty stones. Eighteen of them are grey granite and one is made of quartz. Inside the circle at the south-west is a slanting stone that measures approximately 8.86 feet (2.7 metres) in length. It has an unusual carving which could be a foot or an

Altarnun Stone Circle.

Boscawen-Un Stone Circle.

axe. This stone could be aligned to mark the direction of the sun moving southerly after the Samhain. There is a gap in the west side of the circle, which suggests an entrance or missing stones. Two stones at the north-eastern edge of the stone circle in the ground indicate that they could be the remains of a burial cist. Boscawen-Un Stone Circle is open to the public, with easy access from a small lay-by on the A30 road heading towards Land's End. It has a tiny brown signpost at the entrance leading to a public pathway. Grid Reference: SW 41216 27358.

Boskednan Stone Circle

Boskednan is a partly ruined Bronze Age stone circle that may have once contained twenty-two stones of grey granite. Today only ten stones remain – seven stones are standing and three of them have fallen. The tallest stone is approximately 6.6 feet (2 metres) high and stands near to a fallen stone of a similar size. From the centre of the circle looking towards the north-north-east, the two stones are almost in alignment with the peak of a nearby ancient Neolithic settlement named Carn Galver. There are also two round barrows in alignment. One of them lies approximately 690 feet (210 metres) to the north-north-west, which can be mistaken for a stone circle. The other is partly ruined and is situated near to the south-south-eastern edge. Boskednan Stone Circle is easily accessed from the parking area at the Carn Galver Copper Mine. To reach the stones, walk along the miner's path heading north-west. Grid Reference: SW 43400 35100.

Boskednan Stone Circle.

Craddock Moor Stone Circle

Sadly, Craddock Moor Stone Circle is hidden by the overgrowth of the land. However, according to research by Historic England it is confirmed a neglected monument that is yet to be excavated. According to their research, it tells us that the monument was possibly constructed during the Early to Middle Bronze Ages and consists of sixteen or more fallen stones. Apparently, one of them remains upright. The site is situated somewhere near to an embanked enclosure, Craddock Moor Stone Row and approximately half of a mile north-west are The Hurlers Stone Circles. Grid Reference: SX 24900 71800.

Duloe Stone Circle

Duloe is the smallest Bronze Age stone circle in Cornwall. It is a rare oval-shaped stone circle containing eight massive white quartzite stones. Seven of the stones are still standing, and one of them has since fallen. Each of the stones varies in size. The largest is at the southern side, weighing over 12 tons and measuring 8.7 feet (2.65 metres) in height. The circle measures 39 feet (11.9 metres) by 35 feet (10.7 metres) from north to south. Duloe is open to the public and can be easily accessed from the B3254 road. Follow the signpost pointing to the stone circle. Grid Reference: SX 23570 58300.

Duloe Stone Circle.

Emblance Downs Stone Circles

These two ruined Bronze Age stone circles are relatively the same size. Each of them measures approximately 25.15 yards (23 metres) in diameter. The distance between them is about 8.2 feet (2.5 metres). The stones in both circles are spaced unevenly with the tallest stone standing at the south-east. Circle A (eastern) has eight stones. Four of them are upright and one has fallen on the edge of the ring. Two stones are lying outside the circle, and in the south-east within the circle, there is a slab measuring approximately

Emblance Downs Stone Circle I.

Emblance Downs Stone Circle II.

10.82 feet (3.3 metres) in length. Circle B (western) may have contained fifteen stones originally. Today, only eight of them remain. Six are standing upright, but the rest of the stones have fallen. Two of them lie on the perimeter and the other two recumbent stones are close to the centre of the circle. Emblance Downs Stone Circles are just a short walk of about 984 feet (300 metres) to the north-west of Leaze Stone Circle. Grid Reference: SX 13400 77500.

Fernacre Stone Circle

Fernacre is a Bronze Age stone circle and one of the largest in Cornwall, measuring approximately 152 feet by 142 feet (46.2 metres by 43.3 metres). It contains seventy-two stones. Thirty-nine of them remain upright, thirty have fallen and three stones are inside the circle. The tallest stone measures 4.3 feet (1.3 metres) and the longest fallen stone measures 6.9 feet (2.1 metres). Locating this site involves a long trek from the 'Private' notice near to Mellon Farm. However, assuming permission has been granted to drive along the track, to the left is Middle Moor Cross, and on the right is an entrance to Camperdown Farm. There are two other stone circles en route to Fernacre Stone Circle. Louden Stone Circle is close to the road on your right, and Stannon Stone Circle is opposite (on the left in the far distance). Fernacre Stone Circle is in a field a little further on the left-hand side. Grid Reference: SX 14470 79970.

Fernacre Stone Circle.

Goodaver Stone Circle

Goodaver is a Bronze Age stone circle that was discovered in 1906 by Reverend A. H. Malan when only three stones remained standing. It originally contained twenty-eight standing stones, but today only twenty-three remain. The circle measures approximately 106 feet (32.3 metres) in diameter and stands near to the top of Shepard's Hill on private land. Most of the stones are rectangular and measure between 2 feet (0.6 metres) in height and 5.2 feet (1.6 metres) by 1.45 feet (0.44 metres) wide. The spaces between the stones are approximately 12 feet (3.7 metres) and aligned to other large Bodmin Moor circles.

Goodaver Stone Circle.

Soon after the discovery, the local farmers attempted to restore the monument by supplying their workers. Unfortunately, they failed miserably to replicate the original circle. Several of the stones are spaced incorrectly and stand in the wrong places. Some of them are even upside down and facing the wrong way round. Goodaver Stone Circle is surrounded by private land at the top of a steep hill. Permission may be granted at the nearest farmhouse but is difficult to get to. Grid Reference: SX 20850 75150.

The Hurlers Stone Circles

The Hurlers are a set of three Bronze Age stone circles managed by the Cornwall Heritage Trust on behalf of English Heritage. The circles stand in a straight line from the south-west to the north-east. Circle A is the southern outer ring consisting of nine stones placed in a circular diameter of 115 feet (35 metres). Seven stones are partially buried. Two of them are still standing. Circle B is the slightly elliptical centre ring. It is the largest, measuring 138 feet (142 metres) in diameter. The circle may have contained twenty-eight stones when first erected, but today only fourteen of them remain. Circle C is the northern outer ring. It has a circular diameter of 108 feet (33 metres). There once stood thirty stones but only fifteen remain. There are two monoliths known as 'the Pipers' standing 330 feet (100 metres) south-west of the middle circle that could be the entrance to the monument. The Hurlers are signposted just a short walk away from the parking area at Minions village. There is also an interesting information board for public viewing. Grid Reference: SX 25792 71669.

The Hurlers Stone Circles.

Leaze Stone Circle.

Leaze Stone Circle

This Bronze Age stone circle consists of sixteen granite stones measuring approximately 4 feet (1.22 metres) high and 1.64 feet (0.5 metres) wide. There may have been twenty-two stones originally. Today ten stones are still standing, and six of them have fallen. Evidence of two depressions in the ground suggests when first constructed, there may have been three stones standing outside of the circle, but today only one of them remains. The circle measures approximately 24 metres in diameter and is split into two halves by a hedge running through the centre. Leaze Stone Circle is situated in a farmer's field behind the parking area at De Lank Waterworks. Permission may be required to gain access. Approximately 984 feet (300 metres) to the south-east are Emblance Down Stone Circles. Grid Reference: SX 13660 77280.

Louden Stone Circle

Louden Stone Circle was built during the Bronze Age and is still unexcavated. It is one of the largest in Cornwall, measuring approximately 47.6 yards (45.5 metres) north-south by 47 yards (43 metres) east-west. Although most of the stones have fallen and some of the stones are missing due to robbery, this stone circle is remarkably well preserved. The remaining upright stones measure approximately 1.3 feet (0.4 metres) to 3.29 feet (1 metre) high. The tallest stone leans to the south on the circle's southern edge. The smallest stone measures nearly 4 inches (0.1 metres) in height and stands at the east-south-east side of the circle. The recumbent stones are almost the same size, measuring up to 0.75 metres long. Calculations indicate that the stone circle could have originally contained between thirty-three and thirty-nine stones. Most of the spaces between the stones measure 9.8–16 feet (3 to 5 metres) apart in the northern, southern and western parts of the circle. However, there are minor variations due to the directions in which the recumbent slabs fell. Some have larger spaces due to the stones which are missing due to robbery. At the eastern side of the circle, it is quite evident as the distance between each stone measures between 46 and 78.7 feet (14 and 24 metres). Leaze Stone Circle is situated about halfway along Roughtor Road and can be easily accessed. Grid Reference: SX 13200 79500.

Merry Maidens Stone Circle

This Neolithic stone circle has a diameter of almost 78 feet (24 metres), containing nineteen granite stones which are approximately 4 feet (1.2 metres) in height. The tallest stone measures 4 feet 7 inches (1.4 metres) high. The stones are standing within 10 and 13 feet (3 to 4 metres) away from each other at the west side of the circle and have a larger space between the stones on the east side. Merry Maidens Stone Circle is signposted and accessed from the small parking area on the B3315 road heading from Land's End to Newlyn. Grid Reference: SW 43269 24505.

Merry Maidens Stone Circle.

Stannon Stone Circle.

Stannon Stone Circle

Stannon Stone Circle was built during the Late Neolithic and Early Bronze Ages. It is similar in design to Fernacre Stone Circle (flattened on the north side). The monument contains eighty-three stones. Forty-seven of them are upright and thirty are lying down, in a circle measuring approximately 140 feet (42.6 metres) by 133 feet (40.5 metres). The stones are roughly similar in size, each of them measuring about 1.6 feet (0.5 metres), and one larger stone of about 3.9 feet (1.2 metres) wide. Inside the circle there are two stones evenly spaced, and four jagged stones positioned away from them towards the outer ring. Stannon Stone Circle is easily accessed from the parking area opposite the quarry at Roughtor Road. Grid Reference: SX 12572 80026.

Stripple Stones

Stripple Stones is a 'henge' type of Stone Circle designed and constructed during the Neolithic and Bronze Ages. Measuring from the henge, the site is approximately 175 feet (53 metres) in diameter. The circle is 145.5 feet (44.3 metres) in diameter and contains fifteen granite stones. Four of them are still standing upright, while the rest of them have fallen. A large stone lies fallen in the centre of the circle that has split into three places. It measures approximately 12 feet (3.7 metres) long and 5 feet (1.5 metres) at the widest

Stripple Stone Circle.

point. Stripple Stones Stone Circle can be seen from Trippet Stone Circle looking towards Hawk's Tor and the farm. Entry is via the path to the Tor. Using the farmer's road is not allowed. Grid Reference: SX 14374 75215.

Tregeseal Stone Circle

Tregeseal Stone Circle is one of three stone circles built during the Late Neolithic and Early Bronze Ages. Due to restoration and movement of the remaining stones, no evidence of the other stone circles exists. However, the only circle standing at the site once contained twenty-two granite stones. Today, two of the stones are missing. The remaining stones vary in height, measuring between 3.3 to 4.7 feet (1.0 and 1.4 metres). They are set in a circle of approximately 69 feet (21 metres) in diameter. Tregeseal Stone Circle stands next to a public pathway. The nearest access point is via Devil's Lane, opposite St Just Rugby Club. Grid Reference: SW 38600 32300.

Tregeseal Stone Circle.

Trippet Stone Circle.

Trippet Stone Circle

Trippet is a Bronze Age stone circle that measures approximately 108 feet (33 metres) in diameter. It contains twelve stones, eight of which are still standing, while four have fallen. There may have been twenty-six stones originally. Near the centre is a modern standing stone erected in the nineteenth century which marks the boundary and is not part of the circle. Trippet Stone Circle is located next to a track leading to Hawks Tor Farm. Stripple Stone Circle is situated between the farm and Hawks Tor. There is no public access beyond the farm entrance. Grid Reference: SX 13110 75010.

DEVON

Brisworthy Stone Circle

Brisworthy is a Bronze Age Stone Circle restored in 1909. It is sited nearly 984 feet (300 metres) from the Ringmoor Stone Row and Cairn at Upper Plym Valley. The circle is slightly 'egg-shaped', measuring approximately 78.4 feet (24 metres) in diameter, and contains twenty-four stones, each about 3.3 feet (1 metre) in height. There may have been forty-eight stones originally. Brisworthy Stone Circle can be easily accessed either via the public footpath from Brisworthy Farm, or from Ringmoor Stone Circle. Grid Reference: SX 56400 65400.

Brisworthy Stone Circle.

Fernworthy Stone Circle

This Bronze Age stone circle is situated in Fernworthy Forest. It is part of a complex surrounded by five cairns and two double stone rows. The circle measures approximately 65.1 feet (20 metres) in diameter and contains twenty-seven stones. Each of them measure no more than 3.6 feet (1.1 metres) tall. At the northern end of the stone circle is a double stone row that has more than forty-nine tiny stones along each row. Most of these are now buried along the southern part. A small cairn survives at the end. Situated at the southern side of the stone circle are two other alignments. These include another stone row on the eastern side measuring approximately 67.2 feet (20.5 metres), which leads to a small cairn with a cist. Upon excavations, archaeologists from the Dartmoor Exploration

Fernworthy Stone Circle.

Committee found large amounts of burnt bone and wood charcoal inside it. They also discovered that the original ground surface of the entire stone circle was covered with a layer of wood charcoal. On the western side there is another stone row approximately 101 feet (31 metres) in length, with a small ring cairn at the end of it. Further south-east of the stone circle is another cairn, standing on a high embankment. The easiest route to Fernworthy Stone Circle is at the furthest point of the Fernworthy Reservoir Forest. Go past the car park and you will find room for parking near to the end of the track. Grid Reference: SX65480 84110.

Grey Wethers Stone Circles

Grey Wethers is two Bronze Age stone circles standing about 16 feet (5 metres) apart on a high plain, north of the village of Postmoor, Dartmoor. Each circle has a diameter of approximately 108 feet (33 metres) and are both aligned almost precisely north to south from the centre. There are twenty stones in the north circle and twenty-nine stones in the south circle. All of them measure between 3.9 and 4.6 feet (1.2 and 1.4 metres) high. In 1898 the site was excavated. Charcoal fragments were found and then restored eleven years later. Visiting this site involves a long trek from Fernworthy Forest. My advice is to prepare for a long day out with dry weather conditions. Park at the car park in Fernworthy Forest and begin at Fernworthy Stone Circle, then head to Grey Wethers, and end at Sittaford Stone Circle. Grid References: Grey Wethers Stone Circle I – SX 63893 83114, Grey Wethers Stone Circle II – SX 63892 83104, and Sittaford Stone Circle – SX 63010 82810.

Grey Wethers Stone Circles.

Hexworthy Stone Circle.

Hexworthy Stone Circle

Hexworthy is a ruined Bronze Age stone circle. According to research by English Heritage, a 1904 excavation by the Dartmoor Exploration Committee found evidence that the site was originally covered in charcoal. The original circle would have measured approximately 82 feet (25 metres) in diameter. Sadly, all that remains today are five upright granite slabs, up to 4.75 feet (1.45 metres) high, which stand upright on the south-western side of the slope. Another six are lying down and appear to have fallen. The outer lying stone is a triangular shaped block measuring about 2.82 feet (0.86 metres), which stands 2.78 feet (85 metres) south-east of the stone circle. Sadly, the site has been robbed of stones, which are probably now part of the stone walling. Hexworthy Stone Circle is situated on the northern side of Down Ridge. The easiest access route is via the public footpath. Head on uphill, following the stone walling and barb-wire fencing. There is a parking area next to the cattle grid (on the road towards Sherberton Farm). Grid Reference: SX 56464 65486.

Hingston Hill Stone Circle

Hingston Hill Stone Circle is an impressive Bronze Age monument containing twenty-four granite stones that are between 11.8 inches and 3.3 feet (0.3 and 1 metre) tall. It also has a ruined cairn in the centre with a stone row connected to the outer ring. The circle is almost 38 feet (11.5 metres) in diameter, and the cairn measures approximately 26 feet (8 metres) in diameter. The stone row is about 345.6 yards (316 metres) long and contains 177 stones. The tallest stones stand at each end of the row. The fallen stones were re-erected by Reverend

Hingston Hill Stone Circle.

Sabine Baring-Gould and his friend Robert Burnard in 1890. Reaching this complex involves a long walk uphill but well worth the effort. The nearest access point is from the furthest parking area at Burrator Reservoir, Sheepstor. Grid Reference: SX 58700 69400.

Little Hound Tor Stone Circle

Little Hound Tor Stone Circle is situated about a mile south of Cosdon on Whitemoorstone Down. It measures approximately 65 feet (18.5 metres) in diameter, consisting of nineteen stones when first built. One stone is missing and four of them are broken. The remaining stones (including one fallen) are of various sizes measuring between 2 and 4 feet (0.6 and 1.2 metres) high. This site is very easy to find as several pathways lead you directly to it. However, reaching it is not so easy as it involves a long trek whichever route you take. My decision was to head from Ramsley village, passing Clannaborough Farm. At the second set of crossroads, I turned left to Nine Stones, then straight on at the next crossroads to the end of the lane. From there it was about a 2–3 mile (3–5 kilometres) trek but was well worth the effort. Grid Reference: SX 63270 89610.

Merrivale Stone Circle

Merrivale is a complex of interesting Bronze Age monuments. The stone circle here consists of eleven small granite stones measuring up to 1.8 feet (0.55 metres). It is a marginally elliptical circle measuring approximately 61 feet (18.6 metres) by 66 feet (20.2 metres) from the northern stone to the southern stone. Merrivale is within easy reach from a parking area on the left-hand side of the B3357 road from Princetown to Merrivale Bottom. It's definitely worth exploring if you have plenty of free time to visit. Grid Reference: SX 55350 74630. Approximately 26 feet (8 metres) to the east of Merrivale Circle is another site with a

Merrivale Stone Circle.

much taller stone standing, with an array of tiny stones surrounding it. Grid Reference: SX 55360 74590. There is also a double stone row nearby containing a ring cairn. This site is much more impressive than the stone circle. Grid Reference: SX 55450 74790.

Nine Maidens Stone Circle

Nine Maidens is a tiny stone circle built during the Bronze Age. It measures approximately 21 feet (6.4 metres) in diameter and consists of sixteen stones, all of which are still standing up to 3 feet (0.9 metres) high. However, there are missing stones. The circle was used for burials and did contain a cairn and cist which no longer exist. Nine Maidens Stone Circle is about half of a mile from the waterworks parking area at Belstone village. Park up and walk along the track and soon you will see the circle on the left-hand side just below the tor. Grid Reference: SX 61231 92844.

Nine Maidens Stone Circle.

Ringmoor Stone Circle.

Ringmoor Down Stone Circle

Approximately 330 yards (300 metres) north of Brisworthy Stone Circle is Ringmoor Stone Circle and Stone Row. These are said to have been built during the Bronze Age. The circle measures 12.6 metres in diameter and attached to it is a stone row measuring approximately 389 yards (356 metres) in length. Inside the circle is a cairn which, like many other stone circles, has been stolen. Many of the other stones along the stone row are also missing but the terminating stone further north is still standing. Grid Reference: SX 56410 66170.

Scorhill Stone Circle

Scorhill is a Bronze Age stone circle situated on Gidleigh Common in beautiful surroundings. It is thought to have once contained between fifty and seventy stones. Sadly, over the years this monument has been robbed and vandalised. Only thirty-four stones remain. Twenty-three stones are standing, while eleven of them are lying down (presumably they have fallen). The circle measures approximately 89 feet (27 metres) in diameter. Each stone varies in height between 2.9 feet (0.85 metres) and 7.5 feet (2.25 metres). The spaces between the stones vary in width between 2 feet and approximately 3 feet (0.6 and 0.9 metres). The easiest and nearest access point to Scorhill Stone Circle is about half a mile walk from the parking area at the end of Deave Lane, Langston, Throwleigh, EX20 2HX. Grid Reference: SX 65454 87389.

Scorhill Stone Circle.

Sherberton Stone Circle

Sherberton Stone Circle was constructed during the Early Neolithic and Late Bronze Ages. It stands on a farmer's field in the Swincombe Valley. Although the land is private, the circle is accessible as it stands on part of the public bridleway. It measures 98.4 feet (30 metres) in diameter with eleven stones. Nine stones, measuring no more than approximately 1.9 feet (0.6 metres) high, are still standing, while two have fallen. The stones have been used as gate posts and part of the stone walling. Grid Reference: SX 63900 73100.

Sherberton Stone Circle.

Shovel Down Stone Circle.

Shovel Down Stone Circle

Shovel Down is a ceremonial complex of organised stones, constructed during the Bronze Age. Included is a stone circle adjoining single standing stones, a single stone row and five double stone rows. The stone circle (also known as the Fourfold Circle) sited here is a configuration of four concentric rings. The outer circle measures nearly 29.5 feet (9 metres) in diameter. The other three circles have diameters measuring approximately 21 feet (6.4 metres), 15.4 feet (4.7 metres) and 7.9 feet (2.4 metres). Only six stones are remaining. Three of them, between 1 foot and 2.5 feet (0.3 metres and 0.75 metres) high, are still standing, and the rest have fallen. The closest access point is from Batworthy Corner. There is a parking area at end of the lane next to Hawks Tor. From there, Shovel Down is a short walk uphill across the moor. Grid Reference: SX 65957 86018.

Sittaford Stone Circle

This Bronze Age stone circle is a more recent discovery, which was found in 2003 by a local archaeologist. It measures approximately 111.5 feet (34 metres) in diameter and consists of thirty large fallen stones. Another outlying stone near the entrance may also belong to the circle. Investigations in 2014 and 2016 found that the stones probably came from the nearby Sittaford Tor, approximately 328 yards (300 metres) away, which also close to the Grey Wethers Stone Circles. Grid Reference: SX 63010 82810.

Sourton Tors Stone Circle

The stone circle measures almost 105 feet (32 metres) in diameter and consists of eighteen fallen stones. Many of the stones are missing but the ones remaining would have stood about (1.8 metres) high, with a gap of about 8 feet (2.5 metres) between them. The remains of a granite stone apple crusher sit next to the circle. The nearest access point is from the church car park at Sourton. From there, it's a steep walk uphill along the public footpath. Head along the moors, then up and over Corn Ridge. Grid Reference: SX 54680 89580.

Soussons Common Stone Circle

Soussons Common is situated at the southern edge of the woodland opposite Manaton Common and can be easily spotted from the road. It measures 28.2 feet (8.6 metres) in diameter and has twenty-two stones, each no more than 2.8 feet (0.85 metres) in height. The stone circle is often labelled a 'cairn' due to it containing a cist with two stones. Grid Reference: SX 67511 78692.

Soussons Common Stone Circle.

Yellowmead Stone Circle

Yellowmead is a rare type of Bronze Age stone circle situated on the south-west facing slope of Yellowmead Down. It stands opposite the fields belonging to Sheepstor Farm, near Sheepstor. The monument consists of four non-concentric rings of stones set within one another. The outer ring (1) has twenty-four stones and measures approximately 67 feet (20.4 metres) wide. The inner ring *(2)* next to it has twenty-seven stones and measures about 49 feet (15 metres) in diameter. Next to the most inner circle is a ring (3) measuring 37.7 feet (11.5 metres) and contains thirty-two stones. The stones in these rings measure up to 0.8 feet (0.25 metres) and all of the largest stones are standing on the south side. The smallest ring (4) is almost 17.6 feet (6 metres) wide and has twenty-two stones, the tallest measuring about 2.9 feet (0.9 metres) high. There may also be a fifth ring on the west side which has an arc of seven stones, each measuring about 1.3 feet (0.4 metres) tall. A stone row about 32.8 feet (10 metres) in length leads out from the south-west side of the outer circle. Most of this is in ruin but there are a number of stones remaining. In 1921 the site was excavated by Reverend H. Breton, who restored the stone circle to its original build. He also found a burial cairn within the surrounding circles, but today it is difficult to distinguish. There is no access to this site via Yellowmead Farm. The easiest and shortest route is to park opposite the farm entrance. From there, it's a short walk up the hill towards the Tor, and follow the stone walling and barb-wired fencing surrounding the fields. Yellowmead Stone Circle can be seen with a pair of binoculars from the corner of the hill and easily spotted from the area where you cross a small stream. Grid Reference: SX 57480 67830.

Yellowmead Stone Circle.

DORSET

Hampton Down Stone Circle

Hampton Downs is a Bronze Age stone circle that has seen many changes to its originality. Over the years it has been added to, moved and re-erected. The circle now measures 20 feet (6.5 metres) in diameter and originally contained eight (possibly nine) sarsen stones. In 1965, after surveys and excavations by archaeologist Geoffrey J. Wainwright, twenty stones not belonging to the original circle were removed. The monument was then rebuilt and returned to its original site. Hampton Down Stone Circle is situated next to the public pathway. The nearest access point is from the parking area next to the farm at Portisham Hill. Grid Reference: SY 59600 86400.

Kingston Russell Stone Circle

Kingston Russell Stone Circle was constructed sometime during the Late Neolithic and Early Bronze Ages. It stands next to the public footpath on a chalk mound measuring 98.4 feet (30 metres) in diameter and consists of eighteen stones, all of which have fallen. Grid Reference: SY 57784 87823.

Kingston Russell Stone Circle.

The Nine Stones Stone Circle.

The Nine Stones

This stone circle was erected sometime during the Bronze Age. It is an unexcavated site now owned and cared for by the National Trust. The circle measures approximately 30 feet by 26 feet (9.1 by 7.8 metres) from north to south. It consists of nine sarsen stones with an entrance at the north. Seven of the stones measure up to 3 feet (90 centimetres) in height. Two stones standing at the north-west are taller. One is 6 feet (1.8 metres) and the other is 7 feet (2.1 metres) tall. The Nine Stones Stone Circle can be found in the woodland next to the busy A35 just outside of Winterbourne Abbas. It is surrounded by iron fencing with a gated entrance and definitely not accessible from the main road. At the time of my visit, access was difficult due to the closure of the public footpath. The once 'Little Chef' is demolished and the parking area is now a car sales forecourt. Grid Reference: SY 61077 90430.

Rempstone Stone Circle

Rempstone is a ruined stone circle built in the Bronze Age. Today, only the north part of the circle remains. It would have measured about 80 feet (26 metres) in diameter when first constructed. Eight sandstones of various shapes and size have survived. Five of them are standing and three are lying down. Grid Reference: SY 99494 82085.

GLOUCESTERSHIRE

East Wood Cairn Circle

East Wood is a ruined Bronze Age ring cairn or embanked stone circle situated in the Forest of Dean on Forestry Commission land. It consists of an enclosure formed by a low, rounded bank built of sandstone and limestone rubble. It has a diameter of approximately 80 feet (25 metres) and measures between 16.4 feet and 21.3 feet (5 and 6.5 metres) wide at the base, and 2.4 feet to 6.5 feet (0.75 - 2 metres) in height. Grid Reference: SO 55946 00157.

WILTSHIRE

Avebury Down Stone Circle

This site is believed to be a bell barrow; however, there are six stones here forming part of a small circle. The circle measures approximately 52 feet (16 metres) in diameter and situated in a farmer's field with grazing livestock. Unfortunately, my investigations quickly came to a halt due to a herd of bulls and cows hurling towards me. Grid Reference: SU 11427 71271.

Avebury Henge

Avebury Henge is a marvellous Neolithic site that is owned and cared for by the National Trust. In 1986 it became listed as a Scheduled Monument and also a World Heritage Site. It contains the largest megalithic stone circle in the world and is extremely popular with many tourists, pagans and druids worldwide. A number of other monuments within the surrounding landscape connect to Avebury Henge. They are Silbury Hill, West Kennett Long Barrow, The Sanctuary and Windmill Hill. Although often recognised as a single stone circle, it is actually a henge containing three stone circles. There are two smaller individual rings inside a larger circle.

Avebury Stone Circle.

Outer Stone Circle

The Outer Circle was built sometime between 2870–2200 BC. It measures 1,088 feet (331.6 metres) in diameter and contained ninety-eight sarsen standing stones. Some of these stones at the north and south entrances weigh more than 40 tons and vary in height from almost 12 feet to 14 feet (3.6 metres to 4.2 metres). At the southern entrance, there are two large stones with smooth surfaces, possibly caused by the sharpening and polishing of stone axes upon them.

Inner Stone Circles

A: The inner circle to the north measures 322 feet (98 metres) in diameter. It consisted of four upright stones. Two of them have since fallen. A further three stones stood in the middle shaped in a cove, its entrance facing north-east.

B: The inner circle to the south measures 354 feet (108 metres) in diameter. It is only partly visible because the circle was destroyed in the eighteenth century to make way for village buildings. A massive stone, 18 feet (5.5 metres) high, and some smaller stones aligned to it once stood close to the centre of the circle. The remains lie buried beneath the village.

Recent Excavations

In 2017, archaeologists from the Universities of Leicester and Southampton completed a geophysical survey. They revealed 'a unique square megalithic monument within the Avebury circles', which may be one of the earliest structures on this site.

The Avenues

The Stone Avenues are a series of parallel standing stones that begin at the south-eastern entrance of the henge leading to West Beckhampton Avenue. The other begins at the western entrance. Sadly, over time, most of the stones have disappeared probably to make way for farming. Grid Reference: SU 10407 69966.

Avebury Stone Circle.

Bluestonehenge

Bluestonehenge was discovered next to the River Avon near Amesbury during excavations in August 2008 and 2009 by the Stonehenge Riverside Project Team. Their findings suggest that a stone circle was built between 3400 and 2500 BC, and may have consisted of about twenty-seven bluestones. These stones are thought to be the original Waun Maun Stone Circle that once stood at the Preseli Hills, West Wales. However, at the time of writing this information, research for proof is still ongoing. What is definite is that a stone circle containing bluestones once stood at Bluestonehenge, and those bluestones did actually come from various quarries within the Preseli Hills. All that remains today at Bluestonehenge are the ditch of the henge and a series of stone settings, none of which are visible. Fragments of bluestone can also be found on the surface. Grid Reference: SU 14230 41370.

Coate Stone Circle

This is a ruined stone circle that can be found opposite the Riding Centre. Some of the stones are still there but are fallen and partly buried in the ground and hidden by the overgrowth. Grid Reference: SU 10407 69966.

Falkner's Stone Circle

This stone circle once stood next to Avebury Stone Circle and opposite the Avenue Stone Row. All that remains today is a single standings stone. There are other stones nearby, which can be found amongst the bushes and hidden by the overgrowth along the pathway. Grid Reference: SU 10980 69310.

Langdean Stone Circle

There is some doubt regarding the authenticity of this site. Some researchers argue it is actually a stone circle, whilst others disagree. Could it possibly be just a pile of stones dragged from the surrounding areas? According to English Heritage, no excavations have been attempted by archaeologists. Therefore, with no documentation of proof to confirm whether or not it is a stone circle, the argument will remain unsolved. For those wishing to investigate, the site can be found near a tall post with a 'giraffe's head' along the track close to Cow Down. Grid Reference: SU 11800 65700.

Stonehenge

Stonehenge is the most notorious landmark in Great Britain and, quite rightly so, a British cultural icon. In 1882 the site became a legally protected Scheduled Ancient Monument and is now owned by the Crown and in care of English Heritage (not to be confused with the National Trust, who own the surrounding land). In 1986 it (including the outskirts) became listed as part of UNESCO's World Heritage Sites.

View of the bluestones inside Stonehenge.

History of Construction

According to the valuable work of archaeologists and the process of radiocarbon dating technology, their findings suggest that Stonehenge was built in three stages between 3100 BC to 2000 BC.

Stage 1: In 3,100 BC, a circular bank and ditch enclosure was constructed by using deer antlers as tools to landscape the chalk and soil contained within the ground. While excavating, human bones were found in the ditches, indicating that Stonehenge was a burial place since the beginning of construction. The burials continued for over 500 years.

Stage 2: In 3,000 BC, on the inside of the enclosure, a circle of fifty-six wooden posts was erected. Sadly, over time the evidence of this circle has disappeared.

Stage 3: The construction of a more complex circle began during 2600 BC by introducing precious bluestones and sandstones to form the centre of the temple. The process of radiocarbon dating tells us that the first bluestones came from various quarries in the Preseli Hills, West Wales (a journey of 150 miles as the crow flies), and arrived at Stonehenge in 3000 BC. However, it was not until 2400–2200 BC that the bluestones were erected. Prior to the setting of the inner horseshoe arrangement of bluestones at Stonehenge, these were part of Bluestonehenge Stone Circle, a site next to the River Avon near Amesbury. The larger sandstones (sarsens and the trilithon) are set in a horseshoe shape to surround the bluestones. These massive stones were transported from the Marlborough Downs, a distance of 20 miles away as the crow flies. Each of the stones weighs an incredible 25 tons and measures 13 feet (4.0 metres) in height and 7 feet (2.1 metres) wide.

The Bluestones Quarry at Craig Rhos-y-felin, Pembrokeshire, West Wales.

Alignments

Stonehenge is aligned to the sunrise and sunset on the summer and winter solstices, which are still celebrated by pagans, druids and other like-minded folks. Still to this day, people gather at stone circles to celebrate the longest (summer solstice) and shortest (winter solstice) days of the year. At summer solstice, (usually 21 June), the sun rises over the horizon to the north-east, close to the Heel Stone. At winter solstice the sun sets in the south-west and can be witnessed through the gap between the two tallest trilithons (one of which has since fallen). Grid Reference: NX 36400 44300.

Winterbourne Bassett Stone Circle

Another ruined circle of Wiltshire, it is situated in the field behind a massive single stone standing on the corner of the crossroads, near the village of Winterbourne Bassett. Six of the stones are remaining but have fallen. There are two stones standing at the entrance of the nearby barn which may have once belonged to the circle. Winterbourne Bassett Stone Circle is situated on private land but can be easily seen from the public byway. Grid Reference: SU 09400 75600.

STONE CIRCLES IN NORTH-EAST SCOTLAND

ABERDEENSHIRE

Aikey Brae Recumbent Stone Circle

Aikey Brae is a recumbent stone circle comprising of five standing stones and the recumbent stone with its east and west flankers. The circle measures 14.4 metres in diameter. They stand upon an earth bank with small stones, measuring approximately 5–6 feet (1.5–1.6 metres) wide and about 2.6 feet (0.8 metres) high. The east flanker is about (2.23 metres) tall. The west flanker has fallen, measuring (2.86 metres) in length. The recumbent stone, its flankers and the upright stones standing at either end are whinstone. The rest of the stones are local granite and graded in size. The largest is next to the flankers, and the smallest is opposite the recumbent. Aikey Brae Stone Circle is signposted on the B9029 road, halfway between Maud and Old Deer, with another signpost at the turning onto the minor road. Grid Reference: NJ 95900 47100.

Aikey Brae Recumbent Stone Circle.

Berrybrae Recumbent Stone Circle

A peaceful site situated in a small woodland within 200 yards of the country lane. The stone circle stands on a bank and measures 45 feet (13.7 metres) in diameter. All that remains here is the recumbent and four other stones but mostly covered with overgrown brambles. Grid Reference: NK 02760 57160.

Cullerie Stone Circle

Cullerie Stone Circle is a later development from the recumbent design. In comparison to other sites in Great Britain, this is indeed an unusual, rare monument. The circle measures approximately 33 feet (10.2 metres) in diameter and contains eight stone boulders of red granite. In the centre is a large cairn surrounded by six smaller cairns, each distinguished by a ring of kerbstones. The central cairn is about 11.2 feet (3.4 metres) in diameter and has a double ring of stones. The rest are six single rings containing eleven kerbstones. The outer stones vary in height from 3.6 feet to 5.9 feet (1.09 to 1.80 metres), and some have cup marks. The tallest stone stands at the north side of the circle. Cullerie Stone Circle is signposted and has a designated parking area next to it. Grid Reference: NJ 78500 04300.

Cullerie Stone Circle.

Easter Aquhorthies Recumbent Stone Circle

Easter Aquhorthies is a Neolithic/Bronze Age recumbent stone circle. It measures 63 feet (19.5 metres) in diameter. It contains the recumbent, its two flankers, nine standing stones and two huge blocks settled in front of the recumbent stone. The recumbent stone is a reddish granite quarried from the nearby forest of Bennachie and measures 12.4 feet (3.8 metres) in length and 4.6 feet (1.4 metres) in height. Its flankers are grey granite, each measuring about 8.2 feet (2.5 metres) tall. Eight of the stones are of rough pinkish porphyry, while the other (second stone to the east of the east flanker) is red jasper. Easter Aquhorthies Stone Circle is well signposted and has a designated parking area. Grid Reference: NJ 73200 20800.

Above: Easter Aquhorthies Recumbent Stone Circle.

Below: Inner view of Easter Aquhorthies showing the recumbent stone and its flankers.

Dunnideer Recumbent Stone Circle

The recumbent stone and its two flankers are the only remains of this recumbent stone circle. The recumbent stone measures 9.2 feet (2.8 metres) long, 1.64 feet (0.5 metres) thick and 6.4 feet (1.95 metres) tall. Evidence of a drill hole suggests that it has been vandalised and deliberately split along its length. The flanker standing on the east side measures 3.3 feet by 2.8 feet (1 by 0.85 metres) at ground level and is 7.4 feet (2.25 metres) in height. The west flanker is 3.3 feet by 1.7 feet (1 by 0.52 metres) and 6.6 feet (2 metres) tall. All measurements are approximate. Grid Reference: NJ 6086 2844.

Eslie the Greater Recumbent Stone Circle

This recumbent circle measures approximately 78.8 feet (24 metres) in diameter and includes a cairn that has been heavily robbed. Twelve stones stood when first constructed, but today only eight are visible. Five of them are still standing in the ring with the recumbent stone and its two flankers. The rest have fallen and lie scattered among many smaller kerbstones around the inner and outer edges. The recumbent stone is about 9.8 feet (3 metres) long, and the standing stones measure between 2.6 feet and 4.9 feet (0.8 and 1.5 metres) high. The cairn has a diameter of 59 feet (18 metres) and open space of 19.7 feet (6 metres) in diameter in the centre. In 1873 the cairn was excavated. Archaeologists found a cist with the usual bone fragments and charcoal. Grid Reference: NO 71720 91590.

Eslie the Lesser Stone Circle

This ruined site is a ring cairn surrounded by a stone circle built sometime during the Neolithic/Bronze Age. The stone circle is about 41 feet (12.5 metres) in diameter and contains six stones, although it may have had eight or nine stones originally. A pair of stones are set close together on the south side of the circle. The west stone remains upright, while the other has fallen. The west stone is approximately 3.9 feet by 9.8 inches (1.2 by 0.25 metres) at the base and 4.9 feet (1.5 metres) in height. The fallen east stone is about 5.9 feet (1.8 metres) long and 9.8 inches (0.25 metres) thick and would have been at least 2.9 feet (0.9 metres) tall when standing. There are also two outer kerbstones on the south-west side, measuring 3.9 feet (1.2 metres) in length and 1.3 feet (0.4 metres) tall and two on the south-south-east side. The other stones in the circle have approximate measurements between 3.6 feet and 4.6 feet (1.1 and 1.4 metres) in height. The cairn has a diameter of about 27.8 feet (8.5 metres) with a height of 1.10 feet (0.33 metres). Excavation work was carried out in 1973 and found large stones that were possibly from a cist. The excavation caused damage to the centre, creating a large hollow that is 14.4 feet (4.4 metres) in diameter. Eslie the Lesser is approximately 612 yards (560 metres) from Eslie farmhouse and visible from the left-hand side of the road. There is a gate at the western edge of the field to gain access. Grid Reference: NO 72250 92150.

Image Wood Stone Circle.

Image Wood Stone Circle

Image Wood Stone Circle is similar to a 'four-poster' design except that it consists of five heavy boulders. It measures approximately 13.2 feet (4 metres) in diameter and the stones vary in height from 2.3 feet (0.7 metres) to 4.1 feet (1.25 metres). Thickness of the stones also vary from approximately 1.8 feet to 2.6 feet (0.55 to 0.79 metres). Image Wood is hiding in the woodland but easily located with the following directions. From the centre of Aboyne, turn off the A93 at the signpost for the cemetery. Park up next to the cemetery wall and gates (to the left) and walk up the track through the woods towards the Aboyne Castle grounds. Just before the end of the woodland, go left along a path leading deeper into the woods. Image Wood Stone Circle is a little further ahead. Grid Reference: NO 52400 99000.

Kirkton of Bourtie Recumbent Stone Circle

This a ruined Ancient Scheduled Monument, with only the eastern flanker, the recumbent and two western stones surviving. There may have been six or seven when first constructed but most are now missing. The recumbent measures approximately 17 feet (5.2 metres) in length, 3.4 feet (1.02 metres) wide and 6.4 feet (1.93 metres) high. The east flanker is almost 10 feet (3 metres) tall, and the stones to the west are between 6 feet (1.8 metres) and 7.9 feet (2.36 metres) tall. When complete the circle would have measured about 71 feet

(22 metres) in diameter. It is possible that some of the missing stones were used to build the nearby wall and gateway. Should anyone decide to visit this monument, please take notice of the information sign at the edge of the field. It states that access to the stone circle is provided by permission of the owner, who farms the land. Inconsiderate visitors here cause many problems. If the field is under a growing crop, please do not enter. If you are in any doubt, please ask at Kirkton of Bourtie Farm. No dogs are allowed. Grid Reference: NJ 80100 24800.

Loanhead of Daviot Recumbent Stone Circle

Loanhead of Daviot is a Neolithic/Bronze Age Recumbent Stone Circle built around 2500 BC and situated north of the village of Daviot. Although the site has been partly restored, it is one of the only nine complete surviving circles with the recumbent design. The circle measures 67 feet (20.5 metres) in diameter and contains eight standing stones and the recumbent stone with its two flankers. The recumbent stone and its pair of flankers are placed south-south-west, just inside the line of the circle. The stone standing next to the east flanker has cup marks inscribed on the inner face. Next to the stone circle is a circular-banked cremation cemetery built about 1500 BC and further along the road is New Craig Recumbent Stone Circle. Loanhead of Daviot Stone Circle is signposted along both roads, south of the village of Daviot from the B9001. It is well cared for by Historic Scotland and has plenty of room for parking. Grid Reference: NJ 74700 28800.

Loanhead of Daviot Recumbent Stone Circle.

Loudon Wood Recumbent Stone Circle.

Loudon Wood Recumbent Stone Circle

Loudon Wood is a recumbent stone circle built during the Neolithic and Bronze Ages. The circle is a bank of stones about 11.5 feet (3.5 metres) in thickness, 1.3 feet (0.4 metres) in height and 60.7 feet (18.5 metres) in diameter. Only the recumbent and four other stones remain. Two of them have fallen, but the west flanker is still standing. The recumbent stone measures 10.5 feet (3.2 metres) long and 3.8 feet (1.15 metres) tall, and lies on the south-south-west side of the circle. The west flanker is 7.2 feet tall, and the fallen stones are of similar shape and size. Grid Reference: NJ 96100 49700.

Midmar Kirk Recumbent Stone Circle

Midmar Kirk is a recumbent Bronze Age stone circle situated next to the parish church in Midmar. It has been relocated, re-erected and incorporated into the graveyard's landscape in recent years. The circle measures approximately 56 feet (17 metres) in diameter. It comprises of eight stones: the recumbent, its two flankers and five stones standing on the edge of the circle. The recumbent stone and its two flankers sit at the south-west side of the circle. The recumbent stone is massive. It is about 14.7 feet (4.5 metres) long, 4 feet (1.2 metres) wide and likely weighs more than 20 tons. The two flankers are the tallest stones in the ring, each measuring 8.2 feet (2.5 metres) high. The other five smaller stones stand in an arc to complete the circle. There are also several standing stones scattered

Midmar Kirk Recumbent Stone Circle.

throughout the area. A large thin stone can be found in the wood next to the church and others in the fields surrounding the churchyard. Two other stone circles are close by. Cullerlie Stone Circle is further east of Midmar (near Leuchar Moss woods), and Sunhoney Stone Circle is slightly east of the village at Sunhoney Farm. Grid Reference: NJ 69900 06400.

The Nine Stanes Recumbent Stone Circle

The site is situated between Mulloch Hill and Garroll Hill, hidden by woodland. It is a recumbent design which originally contained eleven stones when first constructed. Today there are only six standing stones remaining and another which has broken into three parts. The recumbent stone measures almost 8.4 feet (2.55 metres) long by 4 feet (1.25 metres) high. Its flankers are roughly similar in shape and size. The western flanker is 6.2 feet (1.9 metres) tall and the eastern flanker has fallen. It measures 6.7 feet (2.05 metres) long. The circle is ovular, measuring 57.4 feet (17.5 metres) from east-north-east to west-south-west by 47.6 feet (14.5 metres) crosswise. The ring cairn is 39.4 feet (12 metres) in diameter and 11.8 inches (0.3 metres) in height. A hole, 1.3 feet (0.4 metres) deep, exists in the centre, which is 15 feet (4.3 metres) in diameter. All measurements are approximate. Grid Reference: NO 72300 91200.

Stonehead Recumbent Stone Circle

Most of Stonehead Recumbent Stone Circle was constructed during the Neolithic and Early Bronze Ages. Sadly, it has disappeared over the centuries but is truly worth a visit. Unfortunately, measurements for the circle's diameter are unobtainable because all that remains are the recumbent stone adjoined by the two flankers. The recumbent stone is about 12.8 feet (3.9 metres) long, 6.6 feet (2 metres) tall and 2.6 feet (0.8 metres) thick. The flanker on the east side measures 3.6 feet by 1.97 feet (1.1 by 0.6 metres) at ground level and 8.2 feet (2.5 metres) in height. The west flanker measures 4.2 feet by 2.3 feet (1.3 by 0.7 metres) and 9.2 feet (2.8 metres) in height. All measurements are approximate. Anyone who wishes to visit should be aware that permission is required from the landowners. They, and their neighbours, kindly ask you to please respect this historic site. They are aware that it has a spiritual significance, so please do not leave litter around the stones, or try to chip bits off them. Grid Reference: NJ 60200 28700.

Sunhoney Recumbent Stone Circle

Sunhoney is a Neolithic/Bronze Age recumbent stone circle situated just over a mile (2 kilometres) west of Echt. It is a designated Scheduled Ancient Monument, one of the best-preserved circles of its type. The circle measures approximately 82 feet (25 metres) in diameter and consists of eleven red granite stones and contains a ring cairn. The recumbent stone is 17.4 feet (5.3 metres) long and appears to have fallen on its inner side. Evidence of seven cup markings is also visible. Sunhoney Stone Circle is hidden under a group of trees and signposted to the rear of Sunhoney Farmhouse, with spaces for sensible parking. Grid Reference: NJ 71600 05600.

Sunhoney Recumbent Stone Circle.

Tomnagorn Recumbent Stone Circle.

Tomnagorn Recumbent Stone Circle

Tomnagorn is a Neolithic/Bronze Age recumbent stone circle situated in the most beautiful and peaceful location. Although it is surrounded by a fenced enclosure on private land, this monument is marked with an 'arrow' sign next to Tamnagorn Farmhouse on the B993. Having spoken with the farmer for access, he kindly granted permission and directed me to climb carefully over his barbed-wire fence, then walk uphill to the site. The circle measures approximately 70 feet (21.3 metres) in diameter and consists of twelve stones. The recumbent and east flanker remain upright, while the west flanker still stands but is broken. Another three stones are still standing, but the rest having fallen. There are also inner and outer kerb stones of a ring cairn connected to the recumbent. Grid Reference: NJ 65100 07700.

Tomnaverie Recumbent Stone Circle

Tomnaverie is a Neolithic/Bronze Age recumbent stone circle standing on a hill of granite. It measures 56 feet (17 metres) across, with the recumbent stone and its adjacent flankers looking south-west. The circle stands on a platform of stones measuring 79 feet (24 metres) across and 2 feet (0.6 metres) high. The recumbent is a massive granite block that is 10.5 (3.2 metres) feet long, 3.3 feet (1 metre) thick and 3.8 feet (1.15 metres) high. It has two cup marks, one on the top and the other on its outer face. The east flanker is almost 6 feet tall, and the west flanker is slightly taller, measuring 6.3 feet (1.9 metres). The circle contained ten other stones when first constructed, but two stones at the north-west side are missing. There is a stone to the south-east that is light grey, unlike the flankers, which are

Tomnaverie Recumbent Stone Circle.

pale red. Inside the circle is a cairn that is polygonal in shape, about 49 feet (15 metres), and surrounded by granite blocks and kerbstones. At the south-west, the kerbstones steer out towards the recumbent. Tomnaverie Stone Circle is situated about 4 miles north-west of Aboyne heading towards Tarland. There is a signpost marked 'Ancient Monument' with parking space on the roadside. Grid Reference: NJ 48600 03500.

Yonder Bognie Recumbent Stone Circle

Yonder Bognie Recumbent Stone Circle was constructed during the Late Neolithic and Early Bronze Ages. It is situated on private land opposite a farmhouse along the A97 from Huntly towards Banff (on the right-hand side as you pass the B9001). Having gained permission from the friendly farmer, I ventured carefully across his muddy land to the site, passing piles of stones along the edge of the field. Sadly, upon reaching the stone circle I discovered that it is now in ruin. What would have once been a huge, interesting monument is now completely demolished. Grid Reference: NJ 60100 45800.

Yonder Bognie Recumbent Stone Circle.

ANGUS

Balgarthno Stone Circle

Balgarthno is a Neolithic/Bronze Age stone circle situated in a public park next to Charlton Housing Estate, on the west side of Dundee. It is enclosed by metal fencing with a gate entrance. The circle measures approximately 20 feet (6 metres) in diameter and contains nine large boulders. Only one remains standing on the western side. It measures approximately 5 feet (1.5 metres) in height. The rest of the stones are recumbent. Grid Reference: NO 35330 31610.

Colmeallie Recumbent Stone Circle

Colmeallie Recumbent Stone Circle was constructed during the Late Neolithic and Bronze Ages. It is now in ruin. Only five stones remain upright; the rest have either fallen or been utilised elsewhere. The recumbent stone is broken and is no longer a piece of the circle. Two of the stones are now part of the nearby dykes. Should anyone planning to visit this monument, permission may be required as it is on private land. Grid Reference: NO 56560 78110.

Balgarthno Stone Circle.

Colmeallie Recumbent Stone Circle.

Templelands Stone Circle

Sadly, according to Aberdeenshire Council's records, this Neolithic/Bronze Age stone circle was destroyed sometime before 1860, during excavations for railway purposes. There is, however, some stones along the railway path near the Templeton Bridge heading towards Dronley Mill track which may have belonged to the circle. Grid Reference: NO 35000 36000.

PERTHSHIRE

Croft Moraig Stone Circle

Croft Moraig is a Neolithic/Bronze Age stone circle situated next to the A827 (Kenmore Road) to Aberfeldy and close to the River Tay. It stands upon a stone embankment and measures 55 feet (16.7 metres) in diameter. The stones vary in size ranging between 2.6 feet and 5.6 feet (0.8 and 1.7 metres) tall. A stone at the south-west is recumbent. It is decorated with more than twenty cup marks. According to the research of Canmore (Historic Environment Scotland), it was constructed in three stages. Excavations in 1965 by archaeologists discovered that it was originally a wooden structure of wooden

Croft Moraig Stone Circle.

posts, upright in a penannular arrangement. The posts were later replaced with eight stones, which stood in an oval position. Lastly, to complete the final stage of this unusual monument, a circle with twelve standing stones was added. This circle included an entrance with two huge outlying stones at the south-east. Two inhumation graves were also adjoined next to the entrance. Grid Reference: NN 79754 47266.

STONE CIRCLES IN ORKNEY

Ring of Brodgar

The Ring of Brodgar is a Neolithic/Bronze Age henge and stone circle built between 2500 BC and 2000 BC. It is a Scheduled Ancient Monument and World Heritage site belonging to UNESCO since 1999 and remains unexcavated. The stone circle measures 341 feet (104 metres) in diameter, making it the third largest in the British Isles. It originally contained sixty stones positioned on the edge of the ring, but today, only twenty-seven of them remain. Unlike Avebury and Stonehenge, there are no stones inside the circle. They stand within a circular ditch up to 9.8 feet (3 metres) deep, 30 feet wide (9 metres) and 1,250 feet (380 metres) in circumference. The tallest stones are at the south and west of the ring. On the south-east edge is another stone referred to as the 'Comet Stone'. The Ring of Brodgar is situated next to Brodgar farm. It is signposted and has a designated car park. Grid Reference: HY 29450 13350.

The Ring of Brodgar Stone Circle.

Stones of Stenness

The Stones of Stenness is a scheduled monument cared for by Historic Environment Scotland and forms part of the Heart of Neolithic Orkney World Heritage Site. It would have been of great ritual importance. Barrows, burial mounds, cairns, four-chambered tombs, groups of standing stones, other single stones and the Ring of Brodgar surround the site within a 2-mile radius. It is said to be the oldest Neolithic henge monument in Great Britain and originally contained twelve stones when first constructed, but today only four remain. The stones are very tall and quite thin with sharp-angled tops, measuring approximately 1 foot (30 centimetres) in thickness. They are placed in an ellipse of about 105 feet (32 metres) in diameter and stand up to 19.8 feet (6 metres) tall. They stand on a levelled platform of about 144 feet (44 metres), surrounded by a large earth bank and ditch. Sadly, these features have since lost their presence to make way for farmers ploughs. The ditch had been carved into the rock and measures about 6.6 feet (2 metres) deep and 23 feet (7 metres) wide. The henge has a single entrance causeway on the north side, and outside of the circle to the north-west is the 'Stenness Watch Stone'. It is 18 feet (5.6 metres) tall and stands next to the bridge in the direction of the Ring of Brodgar. The site is situated near Stenness Village along the B9055 (Brodgar Road) towards Hestwall. It has a parking area and easily accessed. There is also an ancient village next to it. Grid Reference: HY 30670 12520.

The Stones of Stenness.

STONE CIRCLES IN NORTH-WESTERN SCOTLAND

ARGYLE AND BUTE

Temple Wood Stone Circles I and II

Temple Wood, Kilmartin, has two Neolithic stone circles that were constructed around 3000 BC using small rounded rocks gathered from the nearby river. This design is rare and unusual – probably the only circles like these exist in Great Britain. Temple Wood Stone Circle I (south-east) is bigger than the other (north-east), measuring approximately 40 feet (12 metres) in diameter. In the centre is a burial tomb surrounded by a ring of small stones. There were twenty-two standing stones in the outer circle when first

Temple Wood Stone Circle I.

Temple Wood Stone Circle II.

constructed. Today only thirteen stones remain, which are much larger than the ones in the inner circle, measuring 10 feet (approx. 3 metres) in height. Temple Wood Stone Circle II measures 20 feet (6 metres) in diameter. There are only two small standing stones, one inside the centre, and another close to the outer edge of the circle. These Temple Wood Circles are sited to the south of the Southern Nether Largie Cairn. They are part of a wealth of other Neolithic and Bronze Age monuments situated next to the B8025 road at Kilmartin. Each site is signposted and well worth a visit. Grid Reference: NR 82632 97829.

DUMFRIES AND GALLOWAY

Torhouse Stone Circle

Torhouse is a Bronze Age stone circle that has never been archaeologically excavated. The outer circle has nineteen granite stones measuring 72 feet (22 metres) in diameter. In the centre are three upright boulders that stand in a line from the north-east to the south-west. Each stone has a height ranging from almost 1.10 feet (0.33 metres) to 4.9 feet (1.5 metres). The larger stones, over 3.3 feet (1 metre) high, stand on the south-east side. There is also a large stone and one smaller standing approximately 131 feet (40 metres)

Torhouse Stone Circle.

to the south-south-east of the stone circle, and three stones in a row about 426 feet (130 metres) to the east. Remains of several burial cairns also exist nearby. The site is signposted on the B733 road 4 miles west of Wigtown. It has easy access via the lay-by next to it. Grid Reference: NX 38200 56400.

STONE CIRCLES IN THE INNER HEBRIDES

THE ISLE OF ARRAN

Auchagallon Stone Circle and Cairn

Auchagallon Stone Circle is situated high on a hill approximately 328 feet (100 metres) above sea level, overlooking Machrie Bay and within a short driving distance from Moss Farm Road and Machrie Moor. It is a rare Neolithic/Bronze Age site that contains an unexcavated burial mound (cairn) surrounded by a circle of fifteen standing stones. Thirteen of them are sandstones, but the other two are pale grey granite stones that once contained crystals. Today they are no longer there probably due to theft. The site is situated on farmland next to the A841 from Imachar to Machrie and has a signpost at the farm entrance. Grid Reference: NR 89200 34600.

Auchagallon Stone Circle.

Machrie Moor 1 Stone Circle.

Machrie Moor 1 Stone Circle

This Late Neolithic/Early Bronze Age stone circle has a total of eleven stones, set in a precisely drawn ellipse. The axis measures 41.6 feet and 47.8 feet (12.69 metres and 14.58 metres) long. There are six granite boulders which are all roughly the same size, measuring approximately 6 feet by 4 feet by 2 feet (1.8 metres by 1.2 metres by 0.6 metres) and five sandstone slabs in alternative positions that make up the circle. Grid Reference: NR 91200 32400.

Machrie Moor 2 Stone Circle

This Late Neolithic/Early Bronze Age stone circle contains the tallest stones of all the sites at Machrie Moor and can be found between Stone Circle 3 and Stone Circle 1. It has a diameter of nearly 49.5 feet (13.7 metres), consisting of three large standing stones that are 12 feet (3.7 metres) to 16 feet (4.9 metres) in height. Machrie Moor 2 Stone Circle may have originally contained seven or eight tall sandstones. There are two large stones within the circle, one of which has a central hole and the other may have been cut from the original. In 1861 archaeologists excavated the site and found a cist containing a food vessel in the centre of the circle. A second cist was discovered between the centre and the north-east standing stone, but sadly nothing was found inside it. Grid Reference: NR 91100 32400.

Machrie Moor 2 Stone Circle.

Machrie Moor 3 Stone Circle

This Neolithic/Early Bronze Age site is situated directly opposite Machrie Moor Stone Circle 4. The circle is ovular in shape and originally consisted of nine stones. Today there is only one that still stands, measuring nearly 15 feet (4.3 metres) in height (only short stumps are remaining of the others). During excavations in 1861, archaeologists found a small cist in the centre containing an urn with fragments of burnt bone and flint flakes inside. They also found another cist 3.2 feet (1 metre) south of the centre, which contained a crouched burial, which also included some flint flakes. Grid Reference: NR 91000 32400.

Machrie Moor 3 Stone Circle.

Machrie Moor 4 Stone Circle.

Machrie Moor 4 Stone Circle

Machrie Moor 4 Stone Circle is yet another site constructed during the Neolithic and Early Bronze Age. It is situated halfway between Machrie Moor Stone Circle 2 and Machrie Moor Stone Circle 5. It is a simple design usually described as a 'four-poster' that consists of only four granite stones. In 1861 archaeologist 'J. Bryce' excavated the site and found no evidence of any others. A cist was discovered instead of them buried beneath the centre of the circle. Inside was an inhumation accompanied by an Irish tripartite bowl food vessel, a bronze awl and three flint flakes. Grid Reference: NR 91000 32300.

Machrie Moor 5 Stone Circle

Machrie Moor 5 Stone Circle is another Neolithic/Early Bronze Age site. There are two rings of granite boulders. The inner circle measures 37.9 feet (11.5 metres) in diameter and consists of eight stones which are 3–4 feet (0.9–1.2 metres) high. The outer circle has an oval shape that measures approximately 59 feet (18 metres) in diameter. It consists of fifteen slightly smaller stones and one of them is perforated. Grid Reference: NR 90800 32300.

Machrie Moor 5 Stone Circle.

Machrie Moor 11 Stone Circle.

Machrie Moor 11 Stone Circle

Machrie Moor 11 Stone Circle was rediscovered in 1972, found buried under peat, later excavated and restored by Aubrey Burl. The stone ring is an asymmetric structure (neither circular nor oval, neither egg-shaped nor spiral). It measures approximately 42 feet (12.9 metres) by 48 feet (14.7 metres). There are ten small stones, nine of which are sandstone and the other a granite stone. The tallest is a sandstone which has a height of 3 feet 9 inches (1.2 metres). Archaeological evidence of post holes in between each stone suggests that it was at one time a wooden circle. Grid Reference: NR 91200 32400.

Moss Farm Road Stone Circle and Cairn

This Bronze Age stone circle appears to be a similar build to the Auchagallon monument. Unfortunately, it has been ruined at the northern side. Many of the sandstones surrounding the cairn are missing. They were probably robbed or removed to make way for the fence and a trackway leading to the farm. The circle would have measured about 75 feet (23 metres) in diameter when first erected. Only seven standing stones, about 3.2 feet (1 metre) high, remain surrounding the cairn, and another five taller stones stand at the edge. Grid Reference: NR900326.

STONE CIRCLES IN THE OUTER HEBRIDES

THE ISLE OF LEWIS

Achmore Stone Circle

Achmore is a ruined stone circle constructed during Late Neolithic and Early Bronze Ages. It was discovered in 1981 and consisted of eighteen stones that stood in a perfect circle that is approximately 134.5 feet (41 metres) in diameter. Today, only two of the small stones remain standing. The rest have fallen and lay scattered amongst the boggy moorland. Unless you are fascinated by stone circles, there is not much to inspect apart from the views. In the far distance, you can see a formation of hills (known as the 'Sleeping Beauty') that looks like a pregnant woman lying down. Achmore is situated next to the A858 and has a car parking area next to it including an interesting information board. Grid Reference: NB 3170029200.

Bernera Bridge Stone Circle

Bernera Bridge Stone Circle is supposedly a ruined monument situated high on a rocky hill overlooking Loch Roag. There are three standing stones and a (fourth) fallen stone, which are placed in an ovular position and point southwards to a special lunar occasion. In the centre of the circle, there is an unusual creation which at one time could be used as a birthing chair. Previous archaeologists who have surveyed this site claim that it was never a stone circle at all. This could be true because part of the formation may have fallen into the loch and sank due to land erosion.

Alignment Information
Westerly Stone 1. Height: 7.6 feet (2.31648 metres). Width: 4 inches (10.16 centimetres). Thickness: 19 inches (48.26 centimetres).

Westerly Stone 2 (the smallest of the group is placed within 1 foot of the cliff edge). Height: 3 feet (0.9144 metres). Width: 4 feet (1.219 metres). Thickness: 2 inches to 10 inches (5.08 to 25.4 centimetres).

Southerly (northerly) Stone 3 – stands 33.11 feet (10.091928 metres) distant from Stone 1 and Stone 2. Height: 9.1 feet 1 (2.7736 metres). Width: 3.6 feet (1.09728 metres). Thickness: 13 inches (33.02 centimetres).

Bernera Bridge Stone Circle.

Prostrate Stone – lies 9.2 feet (2.80416 metres) distant between it and the smallest slab.
Length: 8.3 feet (2.52984 metres). Width: 9 feet (2.7432 metres). Thickness: 1.5 feet
(45.72 centimetres).

This monument is situated opposite the parking area at the bottom end of the bridge and is
accessible via the gate. Grid Reference: NB 16438 34258.

Callanish I Stone Circle

The Callanish Stone Circle I is indeed an impressive Neolithic site made of local stone
called 'Lewisian Gneiss'. The monument consists of five rows of standing stones connecting
to a stone circle. The circle has thirteen stones and a tall monolith near the centre. Inside the
circle to the east of the central stone is a chambered tomb. Two of the stone rows connect
from the stone circle to the north-north-east, forming the longest avenue. Shorter rows of
stones stand to the south, east-north-east and west-south-west.

The Stone Circle
The stone circle was built sometime between 2900 and 2600 BC. It has a diameter of
approximately 37 feet (11.4 metres), not a perfect circle but a ring covering an area of
406.8 feet (124 square metres). The ring has a flattened east side measuring 43.9 feet
(13.4 metres) north-south and 39.4 feet (12 metres) east-west. All of the thirteen stones
that form the circle have an average height of 9.8 feet (3 metres).

Callanish I Stone Circle.

The Chambered Tomb
The centre of the stone circle contains a chambered tomb measuring approximately 21 feet (6.4m) in length in between the eastern centre stones and the central monolith. During excavations, archaeologists found many fragments of pottery and locally made Hebridean beaker vessels dating to around 2000–1700 BC. Their findings tell us that the chambered tomb was built sometime after the circle and stone rows, which were in use for several centuries.

The Centre Stone
The centre stone measures approximately 15.7 feet tall (4.8 metres), 4.9 feet wide (1.5 metres) and 11.8 inches (0.3 metres) thick. It looks similar to a ship's rudder and stands approximately 2.7 feet (0.8 metres) west of the actual centre point of the stone circle.

Northern Avenue
The Northern Avenue consists of two stone rows standing opposite (almost parallel) to each other from the north-north-east. It is almost 273 feet in length (83.2 metres) and connects to the stone circle. The two rows of stones (east and west) are nearly 22 feet (6.7 metres) apart at the north end and 21.9feet (6 metres) at the southern end. The western row containing ten stones is approximately one third taller than the nine stones standing on the eastern row. The height of the stones from the circle decreases towards the middle of the avenue and increases again afterwards. At the end of the western row stands the tallest stone. It measures 11.5 feet high (3.5 metres).

Stone Rows

Three more stone rows connect to the stone circle. None of the alignments point towards the centre. Row 1: From the east-north-east. It consists of five stones and is 25.37 yards (23.2 metres) long and pointing to almost 6.6 feet (2 metres) south of the centre. Row 2: From the south. It consists of five stones and is 29.74 yards (27.2 metres) long, pointing to nearly 3.3 feet (1 metre) west of the centre. Row 3: From the west-south-west. It consists of four stones and measures nearly 42.8 feet (13 metres) long, pointing to almost 3.3 feet (1 metre) south of the centre. At the time of compiling this information, there is no evidence available to clarify if any of the stone rows were built at the same time as the circle. Grid Reference: NB212330.

Callanish II Stone Circle

Callanish II is a Neolithic Stone Circle within a short walk of about 600 yards from Callanish III, overlooking the waters of Loch Roag. The stone circle would have had ten stones originally, but today it consists of seven thin standing stones. These stones are arranged in the shape of an ellipse, which measures approximately 71 feet by 62 feet (21.6 by 18.9 metres). Five of the stones are still standing in the circle. They are of various heights ranging from 6.6 feet to 10.10 feet (2 to 3.3 metres). Two of them have since fallen. There is also a slab that is lying flat in front of the western stone. It measures approximately 4.8 feet (1.4 metres) in length and is pointing towards a cairn in the centre of the circle. The cairn measures almost 28 feet (8.5 metres) in diameter. Grid Reference: NB 22214 32620.

Callanish II Stone Circle.

Callanish III Stone Circle.

Callanish III Stone Circle

This Neolithic site contains two stone circles consisting of an inner ring and an outer ring. The inner ring has four standing stones set in a diameter of approximately 27.9 feet (8.5 metres). The outer ring contains thirteen stones, eight of which are still standing, the other five stones are lying down. The inner stones are the tallest and vary in size, measuring between 4.6 feet (1.40 metres) and 6.9 feet (2.10 metres) high. The outer stones are much smaller, measuring between 3.8 feet (1.15 metres) and 5.9 feet (1.8 metres) tall. Grid Reference: NB 22515 32710.

Sron A' Chail Stone Circle

Sron A' Chail Stone Circle was constructed during the Neolithic and Bronze Ages. It stands high on top of the moors overlooking the beautiful landscape. The circle measures 2.9 feet (0.88 metres) in diameter and consists of five standing stones (all of them facing each other) and one fallen stone. The distances between them vary from 7.1 feet (2.16 metres) to 32 feet (9.75 metres) apart, indicating a stone may be missing on the north-west side of the circle. The standing stones vary in size from about 6.9 feet (2.1 metres) to 9 feet (2.7 metres) high and 2.7 feet (0.8 metres) to 4.1 feet (1.2 metres) in width. Two stones

Sron A' Chail Stone Circle.

standing on the eastern side of the circle are flat on top. The rest of them are pointed tops. In the centre, there is a smaller circle of rocks measuring 1 foot in diameter. It contains a small slab 2 feet high, 2.8 inches wide and 10 inches thick (0.6 metres by 7.1 centimetres by 25.4 cms), indicating there could be a burial cairn below them. The circle is situated opposite the B8011, about 500 yards (457 metres) south-east of Ceann Hulavig, Uig. The nearest lay-by is about 2,000 yards (1,828 metres) from the stone circle. Grid Reference: NB 22900 30418.

Steinacleit Stone Circle

Steinacleit Stone Circle consists of an arrangement of boulders marking the remains of a chambered cairn. Ten large stone slabs are surrounding a mound in the centre. The site is oval in shape, measuring 50 feet (15.24 metres) in diameter. The true age of the site is unknown but it could be either Neolithic or Bronze Age. Some archaeologists state it was built between 1800 and 1500 BC, while others suggest 3000 to 1500 BC. The site is accessible via the car parking area opposite the lake. Grid Reference: NB 39630 54080.

NORTH UIST

Pobull Fhinn Stone Circle

Pobull Fhinn Stone Circle resides on the south side of Ben Langass overlooking Loch Langass. It is a Neolithic/Bronze Age monument that was built sometime during the second millennium BC. The design is an oval shape, which measures approximately 120 feet (36.3 metres) from the east to west and 93 feet (28.3 metres) from north to south. The circle contains twenty-four visible stones, eight of them on the northern half and sixteen on the southern half, and many others appear to be missing. There is a tall single stone standing nearly 4 feet within the circle on the east side, and two other fallen stones about 7 feet beyond the western edge. Access is via the Hebridean Way footpath from either the Barpa Langass Cairn on the A867, or the parking area at Langass Lodge Hotel. Grid Reference: NF 84274 65010.

Pobull Fhinn Stone Circle.

STONE CIRCLES IN MID WALES

CEREDIGION

Ysbyty Cynfyn Stone Circle

This is an unusual and interesting site containing five upright stones set into the churchyard wall of St John the Baptist Church. It is not known the age or actual location of where the stone circle once stood. This is due to four of the stones not being placed in the soil, yet the largest stone is. Were the stones moved from the nearby field? Or was the church and the wall built around the stones? No doubt it will remain a mystery unless there's further investigation by archaeologists. Grid Reference: SN 75275 79088.

Ysbyty Cynfyn Stone Circle.

STONE CIRCLES IN NORTH WALES

CONWY, DENBIGHSHIRE, FLINTSHIRE AND GWYNEDD BRYN

Bryn Cader Faner Cairn Circle

Bryn Cader Faner is a Bronze Age stone circle containing a cairn situated east of Talsarnau, Ardudwy, Gwynedd. The circle measures 29 feet (8.7 metres) in diameter and has eighteen stones about 7 feet (2 metres) tall. Every stone is protruding outward and upward from the cairn. Unfortunately, the site was used for target practice by the British Army, who damaged and removed many of the stones standing on the eastern side of the circle. Grid Reference: SH 64700 35400.

Bryn Cader Faner.

Druid's Circle.

Druid's Circle

This Bronze Age stone circle measures 114.8 feet (35 metres) in diameter and stands on a low embankment about 2 feet (0.6 metres) high. It consists of eleven large stones, of which ten remain upright, while one has fallen. Four of the standing stones measure 6 feet (1.8 metres) in height. Many smaller stones are scattered around them and rests on the bank. Two holes in the ground suggest there were fourteen stones when first constructed. A large gap at the west about 7 feet (2.1 metres) wide confirms a ruined entrance. Lying next to the circle is two other interesting sites, one being the 'Circle 278' and 'Monument 250'. To visit Druid's Stone Circle, it involves a long uphill trek following the signposts from the bottom of the village. Grid Reference: SH 72280 74640.

Eglwys Gwyddelod Stone Circle

Eglwys Gwyddelod is a Bronze Age circle measuring approximately 26.2 feet (8 metres) in diameter and stands high on the side of the hill. There are five stones about 3.3 feet (1 metre) tall standing upright on the ring. Two other stones on the north side lay almost hidden under the grass. Next to the north-eastern stone is a boulder and at the south-east is a leaning stone. Access to this site is difficult as the rocky track leading to the site is for 4x4s only. It is a one-way system and very steep. Also, there is only room for one car situated next to a farmer's gate on the main road. However, permission may be granted to park opposite the only house there called Pant-yr-Onnen. Grid Ref: SH 66260 00160.

Eglwys Gwyddelod Stone Circle.

Llyn Eiddew Bach III Stone Circle

Although this Bronze Age monument is often described as simply a 'stone circle', it is probably a cairn circle. There may have been fourteen standing stones when first constructed. Today, only seven of them exist. Six of them are still standing and one has fallen. Grid Reference: SH 64200 34600.

Moel Ty Uchaf Stone Circle

Moel Ty Uchaf is a 'kerb' type circle constructed during the Bronze Age. It measures 32.8 feet (10 metres) in diameter and contains forty-three kerbstones. In the centre is a cist. Towards the north-north-east is an outlying stone which may be part of the circle. Three other cairns can also be found nearby. Grid Reference: SJ 05600 37170.

Moel Ty Uchaf Stone Circle.

Penbedw Stone Circle.

Penbedw Stone Circle

Penbedw is a Bronze Age stone circle situated on private land. It measures approximately 98.4 feet (30 metres) in diameter and consisted of thirteen stones when first built. Today, five stones remain upright, and oak trees are living in the place of where four of the eight stones originally stood. The stone circle can be seen from the lay-by on the A541 road immediately after the left turn to Cilcain, heading towards Nannerch. Permission is strongly advised to gain access. Grid Reference: SJ 16600 68300.

Tyfos Stone Circle

Tyfos is a Bronze Age cairn circle situated on private land. It is slightly ovular in shape and measures approximately 77 to 85 feet (23.5 to 26 metres) in diameter. It stands about 3.2 feet (1 metre) raised from the ground and contains fourteen recumbent boulders. There may have been twenty-two stones when first constructed. The cairn inside the circle measures approximately 49 to 52.5 feet (15 to 16 metres) in diameter. For anyone planning to visit, it is accessible via the garden fence at the farmhouse. Permission is required before entering. Grid Reference: SJ 02800 38800.

POWYS, CARMARTHENSHIRE AND RADNORSHIRE

Cerrig Duon and the Maen Mawr Stone Circle

Cerrig Duon is a Bronze Age stone circle aligned next to Maen Mawr standing stone, and an avenue of short standing stones. The circle has a diameter of approximately 60.7 feet (18.5 metres) north to south and 57.4 feet (17.5 metres) east to west. It consists of twenty sandstones of about 1.9 feet (0.6 metres) in size. Eighteen of them are still standing upright, one has fallen, and the other is barely visible. Grid Reference: SN 85120 20620.

Four Stones Stone Circle

A simple 'four poster type' Bronze Age stone circle sixteen feet in diameter, it comprises of four unusual, equally spaced boulders approximately 5 to 6 feet tall. One of them has since fallen. Possible traces of cup marks on the south-west stone can be found but is difficult to distinguish. This design of stone circle is normally found in the northern parts of Great Britain, thus a rare find in southern England and Wales. Grid Reference: SO 24570 60800.

Four Stones Stone Circle.

Pen Y Beacon Stone Circle

Pen y Beacon is a ruined Bronze Age stone circle. Only one stone about 4.9 feet (1.5 metres) tall remains standing. It can be found next to the parking area at the top of the Blorenge, near Hay-on-Wye. Three other stones lie almost hidden beneath the surface, making it difficult to imagine a circle exists. Grid Reference: SO 23900 37300.

Trecastle Mountain (Y Pigwyn) Stone Circles

Two Bronze Age stone circles are situated here on Trecastle Mountain. The largest is ovular and measures about 75.7 feet (23.1 metres) in diameter and contains twenty-one upright sandstones. They vary from about 3.9 inches to 1.6 feet (0.1 to 0.5 metres) in height. Judging by the even spaces and holes between the stones, there could have been as many as thirty stones when first constructed. Next to it at the south-west is a much smaller circle, containing only four stones of similar sizes. There may have been eight stones originally. Grid Reference: SN 83300 31000.

Left: Trecastle Mountain (Y Pigwyn) Stone Circle I.

Below: Trecastle Mountain (Y Pigwyn) Stone Circle II.

STONE CIRCLES IN SOUTH WALES

MONMOUTHSHIRE

Gray Hill Stone Circle

This Bronze Age stone circle (named after the hill it stands upon) is 4,000 years old. It measures approximately 32 feet (9.75 metres) in diameter but could be larger if the two standing stones (nearby) are part of it. There's plenty of evidence here that indicates Gray Hill may have been an important settlement. Many stones are scattered amongst the woodland and mounds and hidden by the ferns surrounding it. The site overlooks the River Severn, making it a clear observation point, either for spotting intruders or communicating with allies. Grid Reference: ST 43800 93530.

Gray Hill Stone Circle.

STONE CIRCLES IN WEST WALES

PEMBROKESHIRE

Dyffryn Syfnwy Stone Circle

Dyffryn Syfnwy is a Bronze Age stone circle containing a ruined cairn situated on private land. Nine stones measure approximately 6 feet (2 metres) tall. There may have been thirteen when first constructed. The circle measures 69.8 feet (21.3 metres) in diameter and stands on the raised ground about 1.6 feet (0.5 metres) in height. Grid Reference: SN 05920 28451.

Gors Fawr Stone Circle

This Bronze Age circle lies at the foot of the Preseli Hills on open boggy moorland. It measures approximately 72.2 feet (22 metres) in diameter and contains sixteen stones up to 6.6 feet (2 metres) high. Eight of them are bluestones (spotted dolerite), the same type of stones used at Stonehenge. Grid Reference: SN 13460 29360.

Dyffryn Syfnwy Stone Circle.